Anne M
July, 19
Evanst

THE INTEGRATED VIOLINIST

BY THE SAME AUTHOR:

THE SIMPLICITY OF PLAYING THE VIOLIN

THE HIDDEN FACE OF MUSIC

THE INTEGRATED VIOLINIST

by

HERBERT WHONE

With illustrations by the author

LONDON
VICTOR GOLLANCZ LTD
1976

© Herbert Whone 1976

ISBN 0 575 02148 9

Printed in Great Britain by
The Camelot Press Ltd, Southampton

To my eldest son Adam,
craftsman and player:
and to all my students,
past and present,
at the Huddersfield
Polytechnic Music School

CONTENTS

	Introduction	9
1	The Human Issue	15
2	The Inertia of the Body	17
3	The Unused Upper Arm	24
4	The Angle of the Bow-hair	33
5	The Little Finger of the Right Hand	36
6	New Wine in New Bottles	41
7	The Many Facets of Spontaneity in the Bow	44
8	Early Music and the Modern Bow	59
9	Left Hand Hazards	63
10	The Function of the Left Thumb	66
11	Co-ordination of Left and Right	70
12	Body Participation	76
13	The Danger of Music Stands and Music	85
14	Mechanics Determine Music	88
15	The Power of Imagery	92
16	The Mystery of Rhythm	96
17	The Breath of Life	100
18	Some Errors in Vibrato	109
19	Portamento and Feeling	113
20	What is an Instrument?	118
	Coda: In Defence of Simplicity	122
	Index	127

INTRODUCTION

SINCE WRITING *The Simplicity of Playing the Violin* I have avoided referring specifically to its contents. In teaching, as in all things, repetition is death, and every lesson is a new experience with a new individual in an ever-changing human situation. Also, I, the teacher, am in constant change, grasping more and more of a sense of wholeness, and discriminating between falsehood and truth, waste and economy, imperfection and perfection. As with myth there is a never-ending variety in the way truths can be expressed and interpreted. What I say, then, does not invalidate what I have said previously, because universal truths are at the foundation of all things and operate in the fields of art and science alike. All this book sets out to do is to present some new ideas and to re-present familiar ones, shifting the accent so that they may be more fully understood; and if material from the *The Simplicity of Playing the Violin* is repeated, it is in the interests of a logical structure and of maintaining a relationship between the two books.

One idea, however, is common to both books—that playing the violin is not just a question of mechanics or of technical prowess. It is difficult to persuade people that playing is rooted in unchanging laws, the same laws that govern motion and dynamics, as relentless and fine as those that keep an aeroplane in the sky or a gymnast balanced on his hands. In the formative years of a violinist's life there is too much arbitrariness—too much is taken for granted and there is little reference to these laws. It is still more difficult to take students later in life beyond the ends of their noses, and convince them that what they do has an equally valid connection with the world of metaphysics. In fact the idea of a relationship with anything outside the violin itself seems to be the last thing to be considered in training. But one of my aims is to demonstrate that beauty and efficiency in any human activity depend upon such an understanding, upon such a relating of lower to higher.

Playing an instrument is like living life: lack of beauty and efficiency in life is due to a man's failure to acknowledge his relationship with the whole—that is, the whole purpose of human life and the Source of all existence. According to the religions of the world, man has become blind and full of error, so that he has now little harmony within him. At the same time, however, it is said that deep down in him is an awareness of his perfect origin and that he has the power to extricate himself from his predicament. This gives him a painful awareness of his present imperfect state, so that he lives in perpetual inner conflict and unease.

Art is very much concerned with this conflict. An artist is a being who is acutely conscious of the split within himself, and his activities reflect in visible form his inner search. He is for ever striving towards the vision of perfection and yet unable to realise it. In the world, too, he sees the same split—constructive energy distorted by violence, and compassion distorted by hate: he is for ever trying to reconcile opposites, and sees only differences, not unity. Somehow, he sees, energy has to be transformed through the elimination of error. In this sense, religion and art are alike—they are both yearnings of the soul and are both concerned with the dropping away of imperfection. At some point the fruits of this may be seen; earlier struggles end in the resolved stillness which we recognise in the life of a holy man, in the late quartets of Beethoven, or in the playing of the older masterly soloist.

What we are saying is that the violinist is no exception—his work is as much a search as the painter's or the composer's. Perfection is the goal and error is the goad. He knows the end but finds the road blocked by apparently insurmountable obstacles. Is it not necessary, then, that he should have a clear understanding of what he is, and what it is that stands in the way of perfection? With such an understanding his work can have a logical direction, and what was once an arbitrary mechanical struggle with technique assumes a far wider horizon. A violinist can begin to see the relevance of integrating himself in order to receive the benefit of the 'gift' of music that lies deep within him.

H. W.

THE INTEGRATED VIOLINIST

1

THE HUMAN ISSUE

THE INTRODUCTION spoke of the need for a violinist to understand what he is as a man before he can satisfactorily approach his art. Wherever we look, in ancient tradition or in modern psychology, we find that man is allotted a basic fourfold division. Most obviously he is a physical being, but within his physical body are three inner faculties which are the mainsprings behind all its actions. These are the faculties of thinking, feeling and willing: a man can reason about a thing, have feelings about it, or he can draw on the store of energy within him to achieve an aim. But in his present state, each of these four parts is full of error—it is working with its negative aspect dominant.

Let us look at them in turn. The physical body is the carriage or vehicle for all our energies. It is of prime importance. An arrow does not hit its mark effectively if fired through mud, any more than a thistledown can alight gracefully upon the ground if it is heavy with water. The body, especially in the Western world, is sadly abused and sapped of its real powers, as we shall see in more detail in the next chapter. The function of thought is to see ratio in things, to make systems out of the impressions taken in from the world outside. On its negative side it is bound to the duality of time, to the need to refer the future to past experience, and because of this it is essentially an organ of fear. Feeling teaches us truth on a different level, through intuition. We feel beauty or pathos; we have a feeling relationship with an animal or a tree. On its negative side it becomes a mere question of like and dislike on a purely sensual level, and human beings are often at the mercy of such feelings determined by the outer world. Will, finally, is the power to initiate action; it is concerned with the mobilisation of energy from the sub-diaphragmatic reservoir within the body, which gives an animal immediacy to be seen in the vertical leap of a dolphin from a short run. On the negative side it is seen as unrestrained anger which ends in disorganised, inefficient action.

Now, of what use is all this to the violinist, who, it seems, has simply to learn how to play a violin? It is very much to do with him because music lives by these four aspects of his being. He acquires a technique through the use of his reason, he moves an audience from the heart through sensitivity of feeling, and he gives a drive to his performance by drawing from his animal energies. And last, he has to train the physical body to be responsive to any one of these three inner faculties. Nothing is possible unless the body is made a perfect vehicle, so that energy is allowed to play freely through it. And, as we have already said, the laws regulating the body are universal ones to do with dynamics, balance and economy; they govern all action and structures in nature, from the honeycomb to the flight of a bird. That is why so much of this book deals with the relationship of the physical body to the inner faculties and to the eventual integration of all four parts. Outer and inner are inseparable, and our psychological and physiological prisons have to open their doors to each other as wide as possible.

2

THE INERTIA OF THE BODY

THE PHYSICAL body is subject to the laws of gravity, and every move we make involves effort to overcome the inertia resulting from these laws. This sounds a grim situation. But it is not as bad as it may seem: the body can actually *move*. The movement with which we are endowed is a wonderful thing and is too readily taken for granted. It seems almost too trite to mention, but human beings are unhappily blind to most of the miraculous things about their lives. 'I am here', 'I can talk', 'I can see', 'I can move', are all simple statements of fact; but which man can hold the magic of any one of these in his awareness for long? We are neither stones nor angels: if we were stones we would have no freedom of movement, and if we were angels we would have no tangible body. But the blood circulates, and the joints are flexible—within certain limits we have free movement, and this, in our present state, is *life*. This is the key to our condition.

The musician is very much concerned in this, for the flexible movement in the body which is life must be developed in him to its finest possible level, and any tendency towards stone, any heaviness or contraction, rooted out as an enemy of his art. It is true, as we said at first, that effort *is* needed in our actions; we *are* constantly opposing the inertias of a heavy body. But the question we have to put to ourselves is 'What interference is there in the body that has no right to be there? How can our tasks be made easier?'

For example if we try to stand on one leg with the muscles very rigid, we quickly find ourselves losing balance. To oppose the tendency to fall we pull back in a rigid manner in the other direction, and then counter that tendency to fall equally rigidly, and so on. Rigidity not only destroys balance, it creates unnecessary effort. Equally if we raise an arm from the side and hold it there with hardened muscles, after some time it will begin to feel heavy; we have to oppose its tendency to drop by forcing it up again. The whole process involves intense effort. In both these cases, the situation can only be redeemed by releasing muscular contraction and by affirming *movement*. We cannot force a balance on one leg; balance is only possible through a constant spontaneous adjustment. (If we try to stand absolutely still on even two feet, there is a tendency to lose balance.) In the same way, the more movement we can sense in the raised arm, the more easy will it be to keep it held there comfortably and for a longer period of time.

There must be the possibility of movement everywhere in the body. When the head turns it should do so like the detachable head of a Russian doll on its knife-edge; when the arm is pulled out from the side it should yield at the shoulder with the ease of a puppet on a thread; when the bow is held above the string, a touch on the arm should be enough to give movement to it in any direction.

But there is another factor to consider: how we *feel* psychologically. If we feel flat, we are heavy in our bodies: we have to key ourselves up inwardly to be alive in our bodies. The reason for the insensitivity of the body is closely related to man's general psychological condition; for along with the gradual loss of his subtle powers, an increasing sense of isolation has arisen, a struggle to hold on to an identity, and a need for self-protection. The gestures of Western man indicate such inner states. They are gestures of defence, fear and acquisitiveness, and are the signature of his condition, with a common denominator—*contraction*. They are the very opposite gestures to those of giving away or opening out; they take, hold and protect. For instance, fear starts very early in life. From the very beginning, in childhood, safety is unnaturally stressed. When a child walks on a high wall with a drop on the other side, the anxious attitude of the parent soon induces a state of apprehension and a tightening of the muscles. And this reaction in similar situations gets more and more ingrained throughout life. Or there is the effect of the change from an inner to an outer awareness. Where human beings were once sensitive in their feelings to the world of nature, now they hold on to it, control it as though it were a possession. The eyes no longer look inwards for understanding. Like the limbs we have talked about, the eyes have become fixed and immobilised. The outer world has fascinated and at the same time fastened. With such dangers on his doorstep, unless a child has been given help in the right direction from the beginning, by the time of his teens, the power in his body has already been asphyxiated. To make good violinists we have to start undoing many childhood knots.

But the question arises: How can a person be helped to re-sensitise his body, to be made aware of it in a new way? It is certainly not by getting him to think about it. The answer lies in two words: *sensing* and *letting*. We have said that man's faculties have become debased—that his ideas have become mere personal opinions, that his feelings run headlong out of control, and that his energy is seen as violence used to the end of self-gain; and now we are saying that the body is a machine out of condition. In all that has gone wrong we see the same common factor: everything has been turned outwards. So it follows that in any attempt at correction we have to turn back *inwards*. The body is wise—it would know what to do *if we were able to let it*. We have to let it teach us from inside so that we become awake to its *sensation*. It has its own life, but can we let that operate without forcing ourselves upon it and putting it in irons? To make headway in this we have to change our approach from 'I do' to 'let it be done'. This change of concept is the key to bodily control. *Let* the movement happen.

For some this is difficult in the beginning. But one way we can be helped is by imagining a strong outside force, such as a magnet, drawing a limb out from the body. If the imagining of the power is sufficiently intense, an arm yields effortlessly from the shoulder; and the experience, moreover, is a totally new one, for we do not feel to be doing the work ourselves. Nevertheless, we may still wish to be convinced of our experience by reverting to our normal practice of *pushing out* the arm, of deciding to make the arm move. Once we have made that comparison there will be no doubt about their respective qualities. There is a world of difference between 'let the arm move' and 'I decide to move the arm'. And despite the violinist's interest in his arms, he would do well to realise this new sensation in his whole body, for it opens up possibilities that operate from the very first moment he takes the violin out of its case.

Another way of helping someone who has difficulty in letting go, is through an exercise where exaggerated contraction and freedom are alternated. For this exercise it is best to lie full length on the floor. The muscles of the arm, neck, trunk and legs are contracted so as to produce a state of rigidity throughout the body, and then, after being held for a few seconds, the contraction is released to give an outflow of energy which gives the feeling of a burden being magically lifted away. The same can be done with either of the arms individually. Throughout, we must remember our aim—to feel from inside: an exercise of this sort is valueless if the body is treated in its customarily external way.

All that has been said earlier about flexibility and movement, along now with this idea of 'letting' as opposed to 'forcing' may be applied to the more general question of balance in the whole body. We cannot enforce a balance on the feet, as we have seen; the body must be allowed to find its own balance. We may now see how necessary it is to remove tension and replace it by movement at all four places where weight is taken and the question of balance arises: at the feet, the knees, the thighs and the topmost bone of the spinal column in the skull. And since the violinist spends so much practising time standing, we will look at these points in more detail.

Balance on the feet is a play between toes and heel: we balance on the sole of the foot. On the toes, we tend to fall forwards, and on the heel we tend to fall backwards, so there is a natural mobile adjustment between the two. Nor can we achieve a balance with the feet too close together or too widely apart: we have to find a distance which allows the possibility of movement. If we look carefully at the balance on the sole of the foot, we can see how the body has been abused, for the effort to enforce a balance has resulted in too much of a slope backwards. Truly balanced, there is a forward inclination so different to what we are accustomed to that for a time we feel to be falling forward.

At the knees, the weight of the body combined with its inertia causes the all-too-common posture shown in the diagram. Such sagging at the knees imposes strains upon the back and the base of the spine, and though it may offer a deceptive comfort, it in no way facilitates balance. With a straight but flexible line between feet and pelvis, the whole cage of the body can be supported freely there. Moreover, bending at the knees symbolises subservience or awe before authority: only an erect posture affirms the self-authority we are seeking throughout this book.

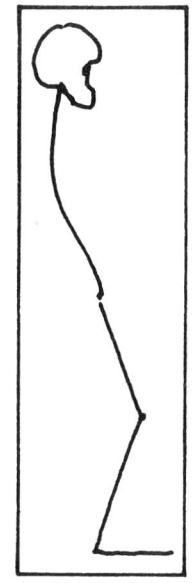

At the pelvis, then, the whole weight of the abdomen is taken. Here above all there is a need for flexible movement: tightening of nerves and muscles at the base of the spinal column is the cause of many later physical disorders. The exact point of balance which has neither too much of a lean forward or backward, gives an easy feeling of the abdomen being poised weightlessly on the legs.

At the topmost point of the spinal column, the head is balanced on the atlas bone, and this, far from being a small factor, affects the whole feeling in the body. Eastern schools speak of the highly concentrated awareness at a point between the eyes and behind the forehead, sending an ambrosia-like power through the whole organism. The physical counterpart to this is the point of balance at the atlas bone between the ears, for if the head is lifted and easily poised there, a sense of release can be felt filtering through the whole body. Difficulty may be had in locating the precise point of balance, and if so, it is best felt as the place between the ears where the head through its own weight falls limply forwards or backwards. From an examination of the normal balance there, it will be seen that the head has been pushed too far forwards, putting the neck in a permanent state of strain. Truly balanced, the head has a feeling more of looking up and out rather than forwards and down.

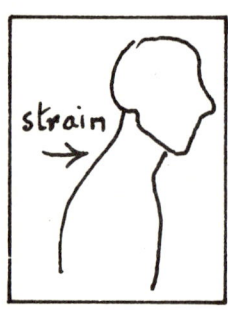

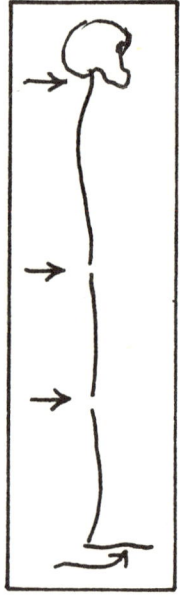

If we succeed in freeing these four points of balance, and in co-ordinating them into one whole, lightness and freedom will be given to all our movements. To work from the feet upwards is to heighten and expand; to work from the head downwards is to unburden a heavy load. Either way the aim is spinal erectness without rigidity. There is little doubt that work on this level has a healthy effect upon the technique of a violinist as a whole, since it allows a flow of power which makes his playing open and vital.

We have looked at some issues involved in the misuse of the body, and seen why it needs to recover powers that have been lost. Aspects of technique that follow should continually be referred to this chapter, for though different parts of the body have different functions they work from the same principles. Our studies of technical issues, in fact, would be best described as 'aspects of abuses and uses of the body'.

3

THE UNUSED UPPER ARM

IN THE chapter 'The Human Issue' we spoke of the fourfold man: the physical body motivated by the three inner faculties, thought, feeling and the will. Much has been said in the author's previous books on how these three faculties are reflected in the form of the physical body, and how they are related to the trinities of the great religions. It has been suggested that the inner threefold division is found even in the arm itself, where the hand corresponds to the precision of the thinking, the forearm to the mediating flowing force of the heart, and the upper arm to the power of the will.

It is not difficult to discern these different functions on an instrument—to see the totally different qualities and problems that exist at the tip, the middle and the heel of the bow. But one thing is clear above all else, that it is all too easy to play at the tip of the bow, and that for most violinists the tip has become a place of refuge from the difficulties facing them at the heel of the bow. This state of affairs, taking our symbolism, can be related to life. It really reflects the poverty of the will, for the typically head-orientated man of today has lost touch with his true feeling and energy resources; his contact with life is superficial, just as the middle-to-tip violinist produces a superficial sound which lacks real strength.

The problem arises for the student when he is required to make a firm sustained sound from the very heel of the bow, and at the same time to control the speed of the bow throughout its length. Usually there is little effective weight in the lower third of the bow, and also a strong tendency to move quickly down the bow to a place of security. Conversely, starting from the tip, when the tone is required to be sustained up to the very heel, a visible paralysis sets in after the middle of the bow which inhibits effective weight from the arm, and this weakens the tone. The ability to feel the same ease and power in the lower nine inches of bow as in the upper half, is one of the master-keys to the violinist's art, and it is an ability which is seldom realised.

Let us take the following passage in the last movement of the Bach A minor concerto, often played above the middle of the bow:

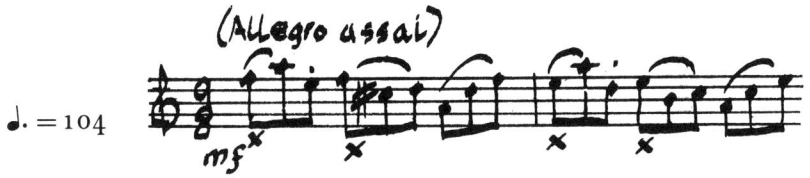

A powerful and broad tone can only be achieved in the lower two thirds of the bow, approaching fairly close to the heel at the places marked with a cross. And in the Bach E major Concerto, the same thing:

The tone during the slur has the correct quality of sustained weight only when played in the lower part; such a quality then contrasts effectively with the quavers E and A which lift through the air back to the heel. It is of no avail complaining that it is more difficult to play in that area: it should not be so, and would not be so if in the beginning the body has been treated with respect and the importance of the upper arm realised.

In this further example from the Bach A minor Concerto, the bow should have arrived close to the heel for the beginning of each of the first, second, and third bars (marked x): otherwise there is insufficient length of bow for the tied quaver, and also a tendency to get further and further towards the tip. ♩=84

It is even more important to be able to control the speed of the bow at the tied notes (marked +) so that no more than two thirds of its length is used. If we do not have that control and fall into the trap of moving down the bow to the 'safe' area, we get the all-too-common effect of a bulge in the

wrong place. It is one of the most difficult tasks facing a violinist to control weight and speed at the beginning of the bow-stroke in such places—to produce a note controlled and alive, and yet less prominent than the first beat of the bar. A useful addition to musical notation would be a hairpin

extending into a line as in the diagram, indicating the sustained control we are talking about.

We have already considered one of the major causes of the trouble in the upper arm—the effect the gripping of the fingers has upon the natural weight of the arm. Another, similar and more obvious, is muscular contraction at the shoulder, where again potential weight is held inside so that the bow only skates superficially over the string. These two basic faults have led to a general malaise in the lower half of the arm (synonymously the upper arm), and as a result, over the years, ruses have unconsciously been adopted whereby its use has been successfully avoided. Often the violin has been made to swing out to the left, or the right hand to compensate by strange contortions of the wrist; or the bow, as we have said, has been pushed quickly down out of the danger area—and all these have been only too successful evasive actions.

The following example from the Mozart Concerto in D major provides another consistently recurring aspect of the problem.

The semiquavers, beginning on the string about the middle of the bow, need to be moved gradually down into the lower part of the bow so that the final four staccato quavers may be played, lifted, quite close to the heel. During the movement towards the heel, in the area where danger from interference is the greatest, the musical sense demands that power should increase, not diminish, as it so often does. Can any passage better illustrate the need for a sustained and uninhibited weight from the upper arm? and how many more do we find like it throughout the violin repertoire?

The upper arm is also involved in the mechanics of bow recovery, as when chords are played in quick succession near the heel in the passage from the Mozart Sonata in F. The aim here is to return to the heel as quickly as possible in order to allow for a preparation or poise before the impact of each chord, and this demands agility of the arm in its movement from the shoulder. The quality of the chords depends upon this move, for the more complete and immediate the return to the heel, the more time there is for precise control and immediate power.

Such inadequacies in the right arm reflect a general human condition, the atrophying of a once immediate and vital animal power—the story of man's divided will. The right arm reflects the power of the will in a man; it is the right arm which puts his intentions into act. He hits out with it, creates with it, and even affirms his power more subtly by writing with it. Men are not equally powerful in the right and left sides: a natural law found through all mythology and symbolism has selected the right for affirming right and might. But that power can no longer operate through the body because of the fear and doubt the evolution of the intellect has brought in its wake; so that a thing of flexible beauty has been turned into an iron cast of the original. Normally in life, where the body is hidden under layers of garments, this state of affairs is concealed, but with something so delicate as playing the violin, the consequence stands out in caricature. Few arms are capable of free and immediate movement at the shoulder—for the violinist the very source of his power. Especially the quality of the sound suffers. During an attack near the heel on a sforzando or a fortissimo note, the tone is often hard and gritty, and can best be likened to the crude and inexpert flailing of the limbs which accompanies a state of anger, compared to the willed energy of the karate expert which has been channelled into ceremonial elegance. Such elegance of action or sound is only possible when there is first free movement throughout the limbs, especially in the case of the violinist, in the right arm.

Before leaving the question of the abuse of the upper arm, it will be as well to note a common error which completely negates its function: the raising of the elbow out of the plane of the whole arm. With the elbow raised as in diagram A, there can be little effectual weight from the arm since it is strangulated by being restricted to the hand and the fingers. This error is all too prevalent because certain systems allow the hand to exert pressure where it is clearly the prerogative of the forearm or upper arm. Such systems

The Unused Upper Arm

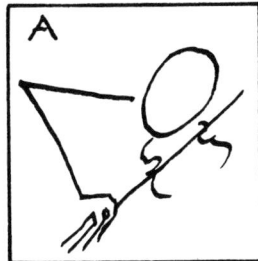

can only give rise to a thin or hard quality of sound. Diagram A shows such a position with a raised and angular elbow, and B shows the serpent-like posture from which the arm weighs down as a whole unit. In position B there is the healthy feeling that the upper arm is a source of power. If we do not respect the logic of this, we are contravening laws of science and of metaphysics; and to those dubious of the possible connection of our subject with metaphysics, it may be pointed out that the gap between physics and metaphysics is, in this age, narrowing year by year.

We have now looked in some detail at some of the misuses of the upper arm. But is there, now, some way of fostering its true use? General exercises, of course, help to free tensions at the shoulder and elbow, but we must remember that if they are of the 'arms bend, arms stretch' variety, little good can come from them. It is imperative to avoid thinking in terms of *pushing through* resistance, and on the contrary to think of the arm or part of the arm being impelled to move in a given direction by a force outside it. Such exercises without the instrument develop a freedom whilst playing which both looks well and is of benefit to the tone.

The quickest way to remedy defects in the upper arm however, is simply to develop the independence of the whole arm from the rest of the body. We have said that the body makes various uneconomic movements to compensate for blockage at the shoulder: either the instrument is made to swing out to the left, the angle of the violin is tilted too far down off parallel, or there is much general swaying. All we have to do then is to eliminate such movements and throw responsibility back completely on the upper arm—to force independence upon it. By taking away such supports, weaknesses will be revealed with the clarity of an X-ray.

In the following example from the Bach Double Concerto the body and violin must both be kept perfectly still. ♩=84

If the player has been accustomed to much movement and he deprives himself of false support in this way, he will find the tone suddenly and unaccountably weaker; he will find too that the upper arm has to work twice as hard to move from plane to plane when crossing over the string or when playing near the heel. Continued practice with the body kept perfectly still will reveal error, develop perfect economy and give independence to the right arm.

At this point a comparison can be made with the human voice from which the singer and the violinist will be able to derive mutual benefit. It has been the author's aim to put forward a logic of the violin related to universal principles, and one of these principles is the threefold division from a fundamental unity. We have seen that technique corresponds to the head, feeling corresponds to the heart, and energy expressed through the right arm corresponds to the area below the diaphragm. And we have seen that there is the same threefold division in the arm too. What is not generally understood, however, is that the upper arm, the lowest section, as with the body, vitalises and permeates the other two levels. We can see this principle clearly in a tree: the root is the source of life, the trunk and branches transmit the sap, and the many leaves and fruit are the highest point in the refinement of the crude energy. The power from the root feeds the other levels; they cannot exist without it.

Now in principle the arm of the violinist is identical with the tree. The weight from the upper arm feeds the forearm, hand and fingers, and at no time is it really separate from them. It is for this reason that the wrist and the forearm must always be free of tensions, to allow the free flow of power from the upper arm into the string. The singer has very similar material with which to work. His threefold division is simply: the diaphragm, the ribs or lung area, and the resonator (basically the head). The error of the singer, like the violinist, is that he often restricts himself to the top section alone, or the top two sections alone; he does not understand that it is the diaphragm, the reservoir of power and controller of the release of one intake of breath that feeds the other two levels so as to give perfect harmony throughout. The notorious 'throaty' singer, restricted to the head, is the equivalent of the violinist who struggles to play a *fortissimo* passage with the aid of the hand, or in a wider sense a player who works only from mechanical accuracy. The equally notorious 'breathy' singer, whose presentation is a flux of feeling, insecure, and with much movement of the body, is like the violinist who uses his forearm—with much apparent activity and a fluid sound, but without any real bite upon the string. The singer who uses his diaphragm is like the violinist who uses his upper arm—he has the power. But for him there is a crucial question. Is he going to spill out that power, ravishing, so to speak, the chest area and the voice box, so that all he has is a massive sound? Or is he going to harness and release it under control, allowing it gently to feed the other departments? Similarly, is the violinist who has power going to crash through all else with heavy insensitive weight from the bow?

To draw upon that power successfully, first the mechanics of the diaphragm have to be understood: there must be no contraction here (this corresponds to the violinist's shoulder), only a natural depression caused by the inflation of the lungs; and above the diaphragm, in the rib-cage and the voice-box, all unnecessary tensions must be eliminated. Then, when air is released under control, the only opposition is a perfectly natural one offered by the vibrating edges of the vocal chords in the larynx, which gives rise to sound. The same thing could be said of the wind-player whose opposition is the constricted reed which has to be made to resonate freely. Power is from below and resistance is above; and between there is no interference. Again this is like the violinist whose bow arm weighs down through flexible fingers on to the string: the bow on the string is simply the resistance to the power of the arm—there must be no interference en route. For the singer or violinist this is the key to purity of tone. After that, it is simply a question of whether the actual instrument, the violin or the cavities in the head are in themselves good resonators and projectors of that power.

The purpose of this chapter has been to affirm the importance of the upper arm. For the violinist it is the root power sustaining all above it. The tree deprived of sustenance at the root will suffer in its upper branches and its fruit. If the violinist is a child, this is almost the first thing he should be taught; if he is an adult it is the first thing he should attempt to recover.

4

THE ANGLE OF THE BOW-HAIR

THE USE of the upper arm is a crucial and obvious factor in tone production, but the angle of the bow-hair, though apparently trivial, also has far-reaching consequences. The angle of the hair as it contacts the string is little heeded, but it affects the whole posture of the hand and wrist and thus the tone production. Like vibrato it has more often than not been allowed to take an arbitrary course from the earliest years.

The most simple of experiments shows that if the bow is angled too far away from or too far towards the body, too little thickness of hair contacts the string. Neither position yields a firm tone. Moreover, with the hair completely flat, giving a wide but thin layer of hair contacting the string, friction with the string is unsatisfactory. A compressed thick volume of hair, in fact, provides the best grip and reinforces weight applied through it; and this, relative to the general posture of the body and the hold of the bow, is only possible with the bow angled slightly away from the body.

Let us look first of all at what happens to the shape of the hand with the hair tilted excessively away from and towards the body. Tilted away (A), there is an excessive curve of the wrist, and tilted towards the body (B), usually at the tip of the bow, there is an angular dip in the wrist accompanied by inevitable contracting of the tendons in the back of the hand. In both cases, weight is forced unnaturally into the hand. For power to flow freely through the bow, the plane of the arm needs to be maintained and felt basically as a line extending from the knuckles to the shoulder (though there is a perfectly natural element of (B) at the tip and of (A) at the

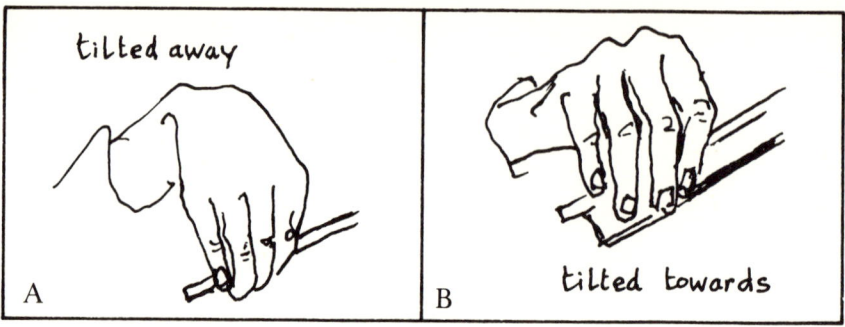

heel). A little analysis will reveal the posture of the wrist, and how this affects the tone produced.

Now if this is seen to be true, surely it ought to be one of the guiding principles of the student in his study of bow control. But we may observe, from the earliest years, a constant change in quantity and quality of tone in legato passages, caused through the varying of the angle of the bow-hair. So should we not, at the outset, study the mechanics of the bow in relation to this simple rule and avoid greater evils later?

For instance, a passage like the following from the Handel Sonata in A major (Op. 1, No. 14), where there is frequent

crossing from string to string, quickly reveals how much the angle of the hair varies at each crossing point, and also shows the tendency to either dip at the wrist or to raise the elbow. If the same passage is played slowly, keeping a constantly unchanging angle of bow-hair, it can be seen how the plane of the arm is automatically corrected—the angle of the hair has determined the mechanics of the arm. The same tendencies can be seen during long sustained notes, where there is a similar correspondence between the transition points of leverage and the angle of the bow-hair. In a down-bow, at the place of transition from forearm to tip, just beyond the middle of the bow, there is a danger of the wrist dipping as in diagram B; we need only maintain a constant angle of hair for the dip to be immediately rectified. And later, if that transition has been successfully navigated, there is a similar danger at the next one where the forearm gives way to the hand near the tip of the bow. Again the hair tends to be angled towards the body with an excessive dip in the wrist, and again this is rectified by maintaining a constant angle of the bow-hair.

Always there is the danger of the power being side-tracked from the whole arm into the hand, and, as we have seen in the chapter on the upper arm, if that happens, if the vehicle for one function tries to take over another bigger one, we have an inefficient machine. Let this significant angle then be given the significance it deserves from the very first lessons in the use of the bow.

5

THE LITTLE FINGER OF
THE RIGHT HAND

NOWHERE IS the abuse of the body more acutely seen, nor the consequence of that abuse so serious than in the little finger of the right hand. With the bow resting lightly on the string at the tip, the little finger is not needed and can be lifted off with no ill effect; but at the heel, the responsibility for carrying the weight of the bow is thrown entirely on to the tip of the finger. This is most clearly seen in holding the bow above the string at the heel, and then removing the little finger. Deprived of leverage, the bow simply drops out of control. Now the automatic way of regaining control when the bow is felt to be falling is to grip with the fingers; this is always the reaction of the body in danger. To some extent most violinists fall into this trap, for when control is most difficult in the lower half of the bow, the little finger is stretched out and tightened rigidly upon it—and in this way an apparent control is achieved. But as we shall see, it is of entirely the wrong sort—it is a mockery of true control, which comes of balance; and balance comes of movement.

The true function of the little finger is to balance the weight of the bow with as little interference as possible, and this can only be done by observing certain guiding principles. First, it should be seen that contact with the bow is made by the *tip* of the finger. Second, the little finger should be kept fairly close to the others, so that there is a sense of them being one unit: to separate the little finger from the others immediately predisposes it to stiffness. Third, and for the same reason, the finger should be slightly bent at the middle joint, because this encourages movement and

flexibility, the key factors in balance. Fourth, in action, the player should be aware of a constant shifting and adjusting of the finger on the bow.

With these points in mind, exercises in slow motion can be undertaken. For instance, by slowly lifting the little finger on and off the bow (for this the bow rests lightly on the string at the tip) we can quickly see any tension hampering movement at the knuckle joint. Such tension and restriction of movement is then best removed, not by *determining* to raise the little finger against resistance, but by feeling it *being raised* by a force above it, the same technique as we used in relation to the arm in a previous chapter. Or again, slow-motion study clarifies the problem of balance throughout the length of the bow. By taking the bow slowly through the air from heel to tip, and observing the changing problems of leverage, misuses of the little finger can quickly be ascertained. Whatever we do, we see that the little finger takes the strain; this is largely its function. But strain is valid only in so far as it fulfils a real function—excess strain is a waste and impedes that function. We are here dealing with science and laws of economy no less sensitive than those operative in the wings of a bird contending with a gale.

Much the same could be said of the other fingers: they are prone to the same errors of tightening upon the bow, though their function is not so directly to do with balance. Often all the fingers spread out in order to control the bow as in the diagram, and this causes visible contraction in the tendons of the back of the hand

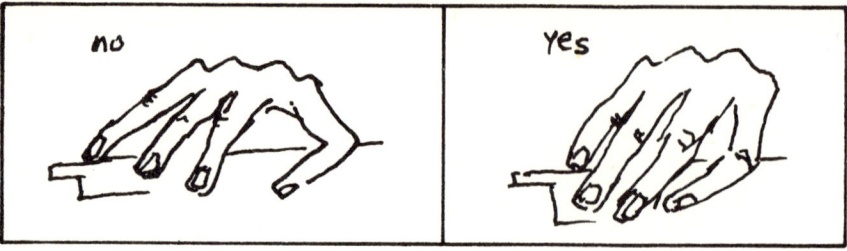

which extend further up into the wrist and forearm. By moving the fingers nearer together we already help the situation by disposing them to a flexible hold. And the thumb is involved in this attempt to control the bow: here too, any hard pressure is as injurious to true control as the tautened little finger. The same questions apply throughout the hand: is there the possibility of movement?—is there economy of effort? The mechanics of legato bowing and all types of involuntary staccato depend on such freedom. And the first obvious indicator of that freedom is the condition of the little finger.

Let us look at legato and lifted staccato in turn. The condition of an even sound in a sustained bow-stroke is an easy transition from the upper arm to the forearm just past the mid-point of the bow, as well as an easy flow when changing direction at both tip and heel. Experiment shows that even a little stretching out and tightening of the little finger causes blockage at these key points and mars continuity. Moreover, the bow tends to be pulled out of

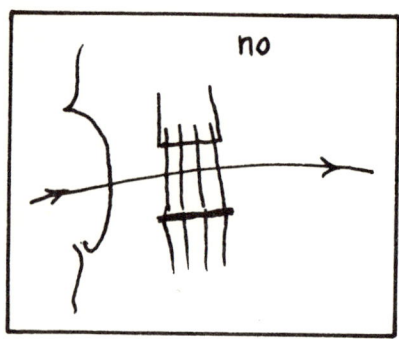

its parallel line, making a curve as in the diagram. Misuse of the little finger is equally injurious to spontaneous bouncing in the bow. If the bow is held loosely and allowed to drop on to the string about two thirds of the way down its length, it bounces to a standstill like a rubber ball. But we only have to stretch out the little finger and grip the bow the smallest bit for that feeling of spontaneity to be destroyed. Surely this is one of the first lessons a beginner should be taught; and yet most players will agree this has not been the case, and that poor guidance has allowed a hard knot to develop which has later to be undone. With the knot undone, the little finger appears to do nothing, and yet what it does is everything. When it appears passively to cushion the rebound of the bow, it is also actively returning it to the string under sensitive control.

Now as we have already seen, it is at the heel that the little finger takes the brunt of the weight of the bow. Control at the heel remains the player's major problem, for either it is not used at all, or, when used, an anaemic tone is produced. So that wherever the question of balance arises the little finger is a crucial factor. In the following example from the Mozart Sonata No. 15 in B♭, the bow

is suspended above the string at the places of the lines, and should be held there lightly balanced, not gripped as is so often the case. (This should be studied in slow motion.) Also, where there is a quick retake of the bow to the heel as in the following example from the first movement of the same sonata (marked ×), a clean

entry depends not only upon the speed of the arm through the air, but upon the bow being finely balanced on the string immediately prior to the entry. Let anyone who is dubious about the importance of the rôle of the little finger try playing these two passages with it completely lifted from the bow.

The use of the little finger on the bow epitomises the whole art of control by yielding rather than by force. In life itself, the more we control by force, the more that force will turn against us. In performing music, when we release control from our*selves*, the music can begin to speak *through* us and not *by* us. And finally, in the symbolism of the fingers, the little finger stands for the physical body of a man. It is the weakest finger, and like the physical body takes the greatest strain. It has to be trained to be strong and yet to remain sensitive enough to assist and not inhibit powerful forces playing through it. Like the physical body, the little finger of the right hand is more important than players imagine.

6

NEW WINE IN NEW BOTTLES

Everyone knows the satisfaction to be gained from clearing out old material and introducing something new, even if it is only in discarding rubbish to make way for new furnishings in moving house. A writer or artist who does not constantly purge his old work hinders his growth, because in hanging on to the past he is stifling the birth of his new imagination. Equally on another level the fruits of the spirit are not suddenly offered to a man; he cannot be illumined whilst old values remain alive in him.

A violinist cannot attain the highest reaches of his art without such a clearing out at some time or other; the old vehicle of expression must be questioned and something new put in its place. Many aspects of the old have been dealt with under their technical heading, and all are to do with the correct use of power; but nothing is more central than the use of the right arm, for moving the bow over the strings is, after all, the central act of playing a violin. Moreover the right arm, as we have seen, symbolises the will of man, and how a violinist uses this arm reflects clearly the quality of his will. When a very young student picks up the bow, his natural aim is to move it over the strings to produce a sound—to *try* to elicit sounds out of what seems to him an unresponsive instrument. The struggle remains with him for many years, and it is this struggle against opposition, this sheer lack of enjoyment, that has deterred many a potential violinist from his practice. The effort to overcome resistance is reflected in the attitudes players have to their instruments. One hears the words 'Something is not right with my instrument', or 'The sound-post needs moving' or 'What a terrible set of strings':

there is always the tendency to blame the instrument and then to attempt to remedy its defects by trying to get more out of it. The result, more often than not, is that the right arm is pressed down harder—it becomes a force being used against resistance. Now we know the use of force in any field only perpetuates itself; the more force there is, the more there is an upsurge of resistance. To use force to achieve order in life, as with the violin bow, only produces a deceptive appearance of control. We have to take the force away and try a new system. Using the image of our chapter heading, we need a new bottle before we can put in new wine.

For the right hand we have to work towards the elimination of interference from the fingers, so that when the bow is raised above the string, it can be held without strain, and moved through the air from tip to heel with a true sense of balance. When this is achieved we have replaced the old bottle by a new one: it is now possible to put in the new wine. And the new wine is contained in one word: *weight*. When we now make a legato bow stroke, we do not press or squeeze as though fighting for something; we affirm a gentle downwards weight of the arm via the fingers, feeling a healthy friction between bow and string. This is the new wine of true violin tone. If we want more, we *weigh* more, we feel the contact more—we do not aggress or squeeze more.

A similar change has to take place in every department: the old bottle has first to be emptied. In the left hand the fingers can be strengthened only by emptying them of restrictive tensions, not by firing them down harder and faster through the mud of error. Here we have to study the source of the power at the knuckles, aiming at flexibility there so as to allow the movement to be immediate and powerful. Equally in holding the violin, we have to take away downwards pressure of the chin upon the violin so that with the aid of well-chosen chin and shoulder rests, we have a hold secure enough to leave the left arm free to move in any direction at will.

Whichever aspect of technique we take, it is aggressive struggle which is the silted-up old bottle that has to be abandoned in favour of a new one so that the effervescent wine of natural power, new wine, may be poured in.

7

THE MANY FACETS OF SPONTANEITY IN THE BOW

KNOWLEDGE OF the true use of the body, with an understanding of the function of the upper arm and the little finger, leads to the heart of bowing technique—the possibility of a spontaneous bounce of the bow on the string. When it is not playing legato or stopped staccato on the string, the bow is in some way lifting off the string as a result of the interaction between its own tension and the taut string. This covers a wide range of bowing in which the lift ranges from what can be described as 'almost completely involuntary' to 'almost completely controlled'—the first as when the bow is simply dropped on to the string and allowed to bounce to a standstill like a rubber ball, and the second as when the bow is thrown on to the string so that each note is individually controlled. The area between these two poles contains a hundred shades of difference, all of which are summed up by a simple dot on paper, and it is the task of the violinist to sense exactly the musical requirements of that dry shorthand. Exactly where does the balance between 'involuntary' and 'controlled' lie, and where is it located in the bow?

First of all we have to understand the tensional characteristics of the bow and the string themselves. In the bow, efficient tension is where the greatest elasticity in the wood is felt, not at the maximum tension level where the wood is virtually straightened out. In the string, the most efficient point of tension to be contacted by the bow is away from the point of maximum tension adjacent to the bridge, about $\frac{3}{4}''$ to $1''$ from the bridge. It is worthy of note that in both cases it is not the maximum tension point that produces the vital spring we are seeking.

With this in mind, if the bow is held lightly, and simply allowed to drop on to the string at a point between the 7th and 8th divisions of the bow (see the diagram on page 51), it will, as we have said, bounce regularly to a standstill: (a). And if it is now dropped as before, but this time allowed to travel towards the tip

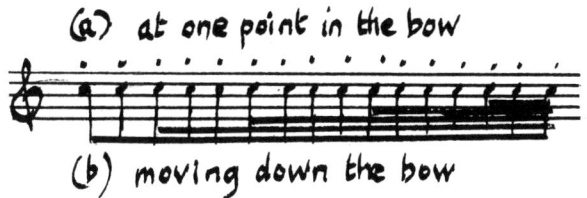

once it has started to bounce, a similar pattern will be produced: (b). In both cases, as the action is purely mechanical, and supposing there to be no interference from the fingers, each note loses impetus after the initial bounce, becoming quicker and smaller as it progresses. (The only difference is that in (b) the bow has moved laterally and produces an actual musical sound.) But in both it is the involuntary bounce that has to be seen as the violinist's great treasure. It has to be studied and valued more than any one thing because it is the empty centre from which all the other subtle refinements of bowing later emerge. Fingers have to be so relaxed that they offer no interference to that free action. There is no other short-cut to the mastery of most of the staccato passages in violin literature.

When this emptiness has been understood, then it is possible to insert shades of voluntary action—that is, action willed by the player. The bow can be thrown on to the string rather than dropped, giving different degrees of dynamic intensity to the original version (p. 46): or sensitive control in the fingers can regenerate the natural loss of impetus and shape rhythmic patterns. We can now fuse our will with the will of the bow, so to speak,

bringing it under our authority in the same way we would control a wild horse, by coaxing with gentle manipulation of the reins, not

by aggressive domination. As the student experiments, three things become clear: (a) that the louder the dynamic, the further down from the tip towards the middle of the bow will he need to play (any appreciable increase necessitates moving from the 7th or 8th to the 5th or 6th divisions of the bow—see p. 51); (b) that with this type of bowing, an involuntary spring is impracticable beyond the middle in the lower half of the bow; and (c) that there is a danger of the fingers trying to play individual notes and also trying to effect the change in direction of the bow, when this should come from the shoulder only.

Much of the lifted staccato we are discussing, however, consists of alternate down- and up-bows, and here, though we are still concerned with the balance between 'involuntary' and 'controlled', quite a different element is introduced. This is best studied by analysing a single note 'thrown' on to the string at about the mid-point of the bow ('thrown' indicates willed as opposed to a passive dropping, the movement stemming from the shoulder). Due to the inherent tensions of bow and string there is a lively spring back of the bow in the air, when it is again in the control of the fingers. (Only about two inches of the bow length need to be used.) But the crucial question is: *How* do the fingers control the bow in the air? Certainly in most cases, control is gained through a *grip* of the fingers on the bow, especially by the little finger. But we have seen that tightening of the fingers upon the bow is not the answer: in the appropriate chapter we saw that control of the bow is only gained through a sense of balance which comes from mobility in the fingers. Here, with the bow held in the air, extraneous finger pressure is an interference, and impedes both the throw and the spring of the note from the string.

The next stage in the exercise is a repetition of the process with an up-bow, again analysing the action of the bow. Finally, down- and up-bows are alternated, and to do this successfully, high-speed adjustment is demanded in the fingers. The aim is now to decrease  the time gap between each alternate bow, until it can be thrown  down and caught at speed with the same feeling as we had in the original slow tempo. Alternated so, the active throw and the passive hold, once felt individually, become part of a whole process, and the mechanics can soon be discarded. The word *spontaneity* can then be used in its true meaning, because in such simple rhythmic patterns as the following, the spring in the bow  appears to come of its own accord—to engender itself.

The whole exercise can now be varied. A sequence of down-  bows is thrown on to the string between the 5th and 7th divisions, involving a re-take of the bow through the air back to an identical point above the string; and the same is repeated with up-bows. (The arrows indicate the circular movement drawn by the tip of the bow through the air.) Again,

the tempo of the sequence is varied until there is continuous movement and increased spontaneity.

Finally, familiarity with these principles leads to the use of a passage of music such as the opening of the last movement of the *Eine kleine Nachtmusik*, taking

individual bars and experimenting with changes of tempo, dynamics and placing of the bow.

So far we have studied the mechanics of a bow thrown down on to the string. But the spring in the bow can also engender itself from flat bow-strokes played on the string, and this is another approach to spontaneity. Such a spring comes, as before, from the interaction of the tensions of bow and string, and again is most effective at the middle of the bow about three-quarters of an inch from the bridge. As in the thrown bowing, its success depends upon the state of tension in the fingers; the spring can only arise if the fingers are free of contraction. Let us suppose that contraction has been eliminated and that groups of semi-quavers are being played broadly and heavily at
the middle of the bow. Now if we increase the speed, the heaviness soon undergoes a change until at about ♩ = 130, we begin to feel the wood of the bow come to life, lifting and springing under the fingers. In short, the bow wants to leave the string of its own accord, as an aircraft wills to leave the ground at a crucial point relative to its speed. This is the element of self-generation again

to which we can truly apply the word *spontaneous*. It is, of course, not wholly self-generated; this is the key to the situation. The player initiates, harnesses and limits that power; he can only achieve rhythmic precision for instance, by interfering with that spontaneity, by affirming the beginning, say, of groups of four or eight notes.

Spontaneity in the bow can thus be regarded in two ways: the single slow thrown note moving to a continuous spring at a faster tempo, and the quick-on-the-string variety, gradually leaving the string and leading if required to a slower tempo. Whichever way, we have to see that the crux of the matter is the state of tension in the fingers and arm. We have to ask ourselves: Is the bow balanced with a minimum of interference?; is there mobility in all the fingers and joints? The reader is invited to grip the bow excessively for the example from the *Eine kleine Nachtmusik* given earlier, to see

how utterly effective this is in killing spontaneity. A little observation will show too that each way has a speed appropriate to itself. In the *Eine kleine* example, the spring clearly belongs to the thrown variety, whereas at a much increased speed as in the Mozart Rondo in G, the bow is best conceived as lifting out of

the string from flat broad notes. In the first example, the bow bounces freely from the string, while in the second it barely leaves it. All lifted staccato lies somewhere between these two approaches. And often, of course, it is necessary to make quick adjustment between the two types, as in the Haydn Quartet Op. 33, No. 3,

where the semiquavers have suddenly to be kept in tighter control and nearer to the string than the quavers.

At this point, two other factors enter into the question of spontaneity, important because they determine the exact place in the bow where a passage is to be played. They are *speed* and *dynamics*. Taking speed first: if we start with the semiquavers on the string (diagram A, page 48) and find the point of spontaneity near the middle of the bow at a moderate speed, say ♩ = 138, then gradually reduce the metronome speed to ♩ = 120, the point of balance shifts so that the bounce operates most easily a little further towards the heel of the bow. If, on the other hand, we raise the speed of the semiquavers to ♩ = 152, the point shifts a little higher up towards the tip. Now looking at dynamics: if we play the semiquavers at a natural *mf* level at the mid-point of the bow and then increase that to a *ff* level, the crucial point shifts towards the heel, and if we decrease it to a *pianissimo* level, it shifts a little towards the tip. These factors, then, cause a constant play, a re-adjusting of the exact point of spring according to the requirements of the music; in each case that point is established with a ruthless predictability, in accordance with scientific laws which have little to do with art.

And yet in studying the examples which follow, the common and important factor is a sense of play or playfulness in the music which is the very basis of art and which arises directly out of the spontaneous lift of the bow from the string. That play depends upon the player discovering *what the bow will do for him* and then gently nurturing that power so that it is kept in play. Is it not one of the joys of playing a stringed instrument to feel the bow doing our bidding without the use of force?

The following examples have been chosen so as to give as wide a variety for study as possible in relation to what has been said. Though due allowance ought to be made for differences in bows and human beings, discrepancies on the whole will be slight, and it is recommended that the suggested divisions given be taken fairly literally. The division into ten has been chosen because

twelve seemed unnecessarily fussy, and eight was not sufficiently accurate; it refers, as is plain in the diagram, to the operative length of the hair. For visual aid and precision, it is preferable to put small strips of self-adhesive paper on the bow above the divided hair.

A   Giga from the Bach Unaccompanied Sonata No. 6:

The semiquavers are played between division $2\frac{1}{2}$ and $4\frac{1}{2}$—best conceived as on the string. The spring is felt engendering itself against the downwards weight of the arm. The elasticity of the wood is felt under the first finger. Upper arm movement.

B Fuga from the Bach Unaccompanied Sonata No. 1 in G minor:

Each dotted quaver is at first best studied between divisions 2 and 6, broadly and on the string. Dots signify the slight lift off the string at the ends and beginnings of notes, felt more as a release of weight than a break. Here, each note is almost totally controlled, and the example is given to show one of the extremes represented by a printed dot.

C Allegretto from G major Sonata—Mozart:

In the descending scale the bow is thrown weightily upon the string between divisions 2 and 4, giving both breadth and bite to each note. The spring in the bow is felt against the weight of the arm, and the whole is contained within a lift of $\frac{1}{2}''$ from the string.

D Tempo di Minuetto from Concerto in A major—Mozart:

Semiquavers at the *forte* entry are best felt on the string between divisions $3\frac{1}{2}$ and 5 (point of contact $4\frac{1}{2}$). A lift arises against the downwards weight giving a characteristic bite. At the *piano* entry later, with weight taken out of the arm, the lift occurs in a more limited area of bow on and about division 4.

E   1st movement, Concerto in G major—Mozart:

The first two semiquavers are of the 'thrown' variety at division 5, using very little bow. In the four up-bow quavers the bow travels up to division 2, with each note thrown separately from the action of the upper arm. Experiment shows the danger of restricting this action to the wrist. A stress on the first up-bow affords a springboard for the three others.

F   Last movement of Concerto in G major—Mozart:

The dots are broad in quality between divisions 2 and 5, due to the slowish speed. As in example B, the weight is released at either end of the note. The bow is poised lightly at the moment of each change of direction. Weight is felt through the whole arm. At the change to the piano marking in the seventh bar the point of spring moves to about division 4 and avoids any quality of spikiness.

G   Allegro moderato from Sonatina in G minor—Schubert:

Ideally an example of perfect balance between involuntary bounce and control, giving a sense of effortlessness. Between divisions 4 and 5 (exact contact $4\frac{1}{2}$) a firm sound is possible, whereas played higher up the bow the staccato is too light and brittle. In the first and third bars, impetus for the spontaneous lift comes from the first thrown note in each group. The very first note of the passage is thrown from about $1\frac{1}{2}$ to 2 inches above the string, and the problem then is the control of the slur at the beginning of the second bar. To achieve this control the bow has to be held in a hairsbreadth pose before starting the next note. This can only be done by slow-motion practice. (See example J.)

H Menuetto from Sonatina in G minor—Schubert:

A slightly faster tempo than the foregoing example, and therefore the quavers in bar three are played higher up the bow at division 5. There is the same sense of buoyancy in the bow, with control and involuntary spring equi-balanced. The first beat of each bar of quavers is slightly accented—but inwardly felt rather than outwardly administered. This affords rhythmic precision. Here, 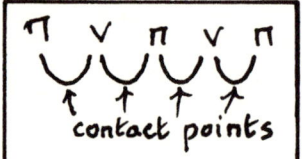 and in the previous example, the movement of the bow is visibly cup-shaped, covering about an inch of bow, and lifting say a $\frac{1}{2}''$ above the string. Each bow-stroke can be represented by the glyph shown. Movement is once more from the whole arm at the shoulder, giving firmness of tone. Experiment will show how tone is impoverished if the action is restricted to the wrist.

I   Sonata No. 17 in A major—Mozart:

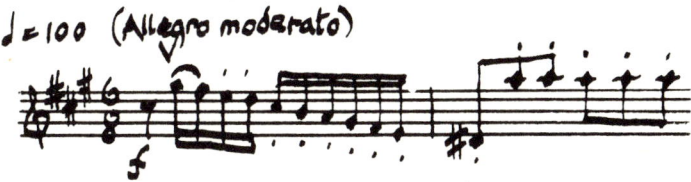

The opening bar is weighty throughout. The very first note starts at division 7, moving through the semiquavers to the 5th division for the six quavers. The staccato semiquavers are best felt as what is called 'on-off'; considerable weight from the arm is countered by the spring of the bow. Movement is from the forearm. For the six quavers, a switch-over to the thrown variety of staccato is necessary; the first quaver has a sharp bite and moves further down the bow to division 4. Only a little bow is needed. Movement is from the upper arm. An instance of quick adjusting from one type of bowing to another.

J   Sonata No. 15 in B♭ major—Mozart:

Again a balance between control and involuntary bounce. The slur starts at division 7 moving down to division 4. The staccato quavers spring lightly and precisely between divisons 4 and $4\frac{1}{2}$. The impetus for the four quavers derives from the F and the G at the end of the slurs in the first and second bars. This example contains a key problem for string players. How is the bow to be made to react quickly enough to control the long crotchet F? The answer is in the still poise on the spring immediately before the sustained note. In slow motion this might be written as:

showing the bow in control on the string before the bar-line. Again, this needs slow-motion study.

K   Last movement of Concerto—Mendelssohn:

In this example the impetus to the lifted staccato comes from the B preceding the six quaver up-bows, and also the G♯ in the subsequent bar, marked by crosses. The notes in question are sustained and the up-bow is kicked off and re-taken within a small distance—say division 5 to 5½. Conciseness comes from short bows and from a vertical lift rather than from horizontal movement. Each up-bow is controlled, but equally the spring of the bow is used. Again, experiment will show the weakening effect of restricting action to the wrist. Action is from the shoulder, weight playing freely through a flexible forearm and wrist and involving all parts.

L   Rondo from Sonata No. 10 in B♭ major—Mozart:

This example presents an interesting study in the difference between the two varieties of spontaneity, the one thrown down, and the other emerging into life from the string. At the indicated speed, covering between divisions 3¾ and 4½, both types are practicable. The first note may be thrown on to the string or it may start on the string. The danger in the first is the tendency for the bow to remain too flat, and in the second for it to be too spiky.

There is a point in each where there is a merging into the other. This is a phenomenon worth careful consideration.

M Rondo from Sonata No. 7 in F major—Mozart:

In this example the semiquavers are not marked with dots, but a lift is implied. At the speed and dynamic indicated, the placing is at division 5 with the bow starting on the string and immediately generating its own lift. The bite comes from using the smallest possible amount of bow. The action is a combination of forearm and hand. Again impoverished sound results by confining the action to the wrist. Hand and forearm work in sensitive conjunction.

N Last movement of Sonata No. 8 in G major—Beethoven:

Staccato is not indicated, but there is an obvious spontaneous lift at about division $4\frac{1}{2}$. In such cases, where slurs are intermingled, it is imperative to move back to the spring-point, the focal point of the passage. These points are marked with a x —— in the example. Elsewhere there is a danger of moving too far away from the focal point.

One or two basic principles emerge from the study of such examples. First, most of the alternating down-up bowing occurs naturally in an area just under the middle of the bow. Second, too many attempts are made to force a spontaneous lift by the action of the wrist or finger—misunderstanding of the true function of the different parts of the arm is discussed elsewhere. Third, the articulation or bite in spontaneous bowing comes largely from the upper arm acting as a *resistance against* the spring of the bow—from the bow and string tensions opposing each other. There is no finer tool at the disposal of the violinist, and it is strange that though our aim is a flow of spontaneity in the bow, what emerges out of that spontaneity is a grip or bite which is the very essence of life. Here then are the three focal ideas in our study of spontaneity—a study which seems unfathomable in its complexity, but is simple in its effect. It is only a pity that spontaneity in the art of bowing cannot be taught when spontaneity is a natural possession—in childhood.

8

EARLY MUSIC AND THE MODERN BOW

WE HAVE just seen spring and bite to be the essential quality of the modern bow, which, as all violinists know, is a refinement of the originally convex and later straight bow which prevailed up to the middle of the eighteenth century. In the period of the viols, such was the poverty of the tension of the bow that not only was there very little bite between bow and string, but the whole dynamic range was extremely limited. Power had to be gained from *speed*: the bow was pulled down the string and a note *emerged* as the speed of the bow increased. A lower bridge without a marked curve limited possible downwards pressure upon the string, and other factors about the instrument all contributed to the limited dynamic range in the music of the time.

Later, prior to 1700, the bow was made of light wood, and, being short, straight and without a screw, had a limited tension. 'Spontaneity' in the sense of the bounced bow was scarcely mentioned. (The 'ricochets' in Jean Rousseau's *Traite de la Viole* [1687] are perhaps the first notable experiment.) In Baroque music, the old pattern still lived: a dot above a note signified merely stopping the bow on the string, and the most common bow-stroke was a quasi-legato, quasi-stopped stroke, slightly lightened at the end, and played over the middle and upper half of the bow. (Geminiani refers to this as late as 1751.)

All these qualities are diametrically opposed to those of the modern bow and throughout this book we have spoken of spontaneity of bounce, immediate impact or friction from the bow upon the string, the production of long sustained lines of sound, uniform speed of the bow throughout its length, and the ability to apply uninhibited power especially through the upper arm in the lower half of the bow. Such changes in musical style and instruments correspond of course with historical patterns: this particular transition was through the flamboyancy and graciousness of the Baroque period to the perfected formal structures and spirit of reason of the Classical—basically, like the change in the bow, a tightening-up process. This tightening is evident even in the transition from Corelli's bow *circa* 1700, to Tartini's bow, *circa* 1740: even in that short time, the bow, short and straight, had become longer and more elastic. And Leopold Mozart's treatise on the violin of 1756 was written from totally different concepts of bowing to those of Corelli fifty years earlier. But the strange fact is that though the bow in the middle of the eighteenth century had become capable of spontaneous lifting through its increased elasticity, Tartini's *L'Arte dell 'Arco* still deals basically only in variations of detached notes, and Leopold Mozart only refers to 'separating and lifting' notes in his pairs of notes played up- and down-bow; though he gives bigger groups in an up-bow, he does not give an example on a down-bow, which is surprising in view of the examples given in the previous chapter on page 46. The idea of a spontaneous bounce does not seem to have been significant at that time. It was only later in the eighteenth century that classical formula gave way to romanticism and the will of the individual, and that this change became embodied in the sensitively sprung bow of Tourte which was to be exploited in the work of Paganini. The bow, finally emancipated, reflected every nuance of feeling (as did vibrato in the left hand), and 'saltato', the springing bow, reflected the freed will of the individual using effect for its own sake.

The aim of this brief commentary is to indicate the difficulties a violinist faces today in playing music written at a different time and for the instruments current at that time. On the one hand we have an alien spirit and on the other hand we have the enormous difference in the potential of an instrument, especially of a bow which changed almost overnight. The present technical aspects of a modern bow, especially with reference to its spontaneous lift from the string, and the motivating force behind an actual performance, are diametrically opposite to those of that earlier period. We can simulate the technique and the spirit of the past, but we are not of it.

The question is, then, what attitude a player is to adopt in playing music of the earlier periods with a modern instrument. Do we, in short, at the opening of the last movement of the Bach A major Sonata lift the two dotted crotchets using the natural spring of the bow with a fine rhythmic bite, or do we keep them on the string as was intended and lose the refinements modern aids can give?

Clearly, ideally the music should be played as it was envisaged by the composer and this involves a full study of everything about the particular period including a study of French, German, Italian and English ornaments, study of original instruments, size of concert-hall, number of players, and so on. We are using a modern bow that wants to spring, and has to be restrained to lie on the string; we have a harpsichord overpowered by strings in a large concert-hall; we have a violin, accustomed to the sustained effect of the pedal of the pianoforte, being obliged to adapt to the clipped ends of notes and phrases of the percussive harpsichord; and we have a bowing technique entirely unsuited to the stylistic demands of the music. In fact we are limited by compromise at all turns. Would it not be better therefore to play without an eye to too much compromise, and when using a modern instrument and bow, unashamedly play according to their intrinsic capacities? We would not thereby have to make a mockery of a Bach suite by spectacular spiccato or excessive vibrato and romantic portamento in the left hand; the spirit of the music will itself determine our use of the instrument, and the treatment of the music, and all would come under the protection of that indefinable element called 'good taste'. But we would at least rid ourselves of inhibition and conflict; we would, in short, feel free to simply play and enjoy the music.

9

LEFT HAND HAZARDS: THE GUIDE-NOTE AND 'KEEP THE FIRST FINGER DOWN'

WHEN WE turn to the left side, we see exactly the same principles and pitfalls that we have been considering in the right arm. Now it is a question of how the fingers contact the fingerboard. One of the acknowledged helps for the left hand is the legitimate preparation of notes in higher positions approached by leap, by

preliminary guide-notes. (The bracketed notes in the examples are established before the high notes.) Equally it is taught that holding the first finger down whilst other fingers are in action above it, works as a stabilising force. These are stock-in-trade devices of the violinist which give a sense of security to the grouping of fingers during shifts to higher positions and to the fingers relative to each other.

But the danger in the early years is, as always, too much stress on security. Often, so strong has been the need for security that the finger holds on grimly and can scarcely be prized off the string. Especially the guide-note is misused in this way and contributes to a general holding down of all the fingers and to contraction and compression in the hand. If such a condition has been ingrained, it is better to re-think the whole process; to think of the fingers making way for each other by a simultaneous take-over movement. Somehow we have to train the fingers to lift off the fingerboard freely and independently.

Such a system can best be understood by the imagery of the term 'walking the fingers', since in a similar way, when walking, one foot does not leave the ground until the other is securely put down. In a passage like the following, if the first and third fingers are kept down, tensions are soon felt in the back of the hand. The

system of 'walking', with even the first finger lifting off the string like the others, immediately counters this danger. But just because increased freedom is advocated it does not mean the fingers should have a straggly appearance: they should aim to return to an ordered position a little above the string, as in the diagram, so that they resemble more the mechanical hammers of the piano. And should intonation suffer through lifting the first finger, it can be replaced when necessary to re-affirm security. The object

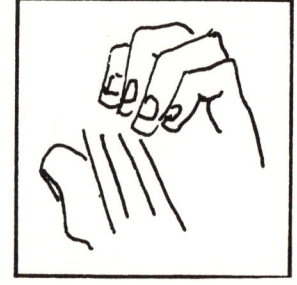

of the exercise is to achieve mobility of the fingers at the knuckles, the source of their power. In any repetitive pattern, as in the above example, the tendency is for the fingers to tighten and to get gradually closer to the string; walking them maintains their height and their power of attack for a longer period. In all events the fingers must be able to release themselves from the fingerboard in a fraction of a second, because the ability to do this is indispensable to their synchronisation with the bow. (See the chapter 'Co-ordination of Right and Left'.)

Besides synchronisation, another reason for high-speed release of the fingers is in the fact that quick adjustment is the secret of good intonation. Undue pressure of the fingers upon the fingerboard is an obvious enemy of agility, making the action of the fingers extremely sluggish, if not at times impossible. In fact, often a student's fingers are so clam-like, so committed to the notes they hit, that no adjustment to intonation is possible in even long sustained notes.

All this and much more comes from the early uncorrected habit of seeking security through excessive pressure on the fingerboard, either in guide-notes in leaps, or held notes under groups. A principle which in itself is sound, has once more been abused, leaving a trail of inefficiency which only hard work can dispel.

10

THE FUNCTION OF THE LEFT THUMB

IN THE right hand it was the little finger we found assuming a surprising importance, and in the left hand it is the apparently inactive thumb that plays a major rôle. The function of the thumb can be most clearly seen by depriving the fingers of its support. However securely the violin may be held between the chin and shoulder, if the thumb is taken away from the neck of the violin, the fingers are unable to work efficiently: lack of resistance to the downwards pressure of the fingers upon the string makes the hold of the instrument and the fingers themselves insecure. With the thumb replaced, the fingers can be hammered down without disturbing the equilibrium of the instrument.

The main function of the thumb is to be there as a resistance under the fingers in whatever position the hand happens to be on the fingerboard. Unhappily, in the early stages the thumb has often been used as a sort of vice whose object, along with the other gripped fingers, has been solely to get a secure hold of the violin. Needless to say this sort of security is false. Consequently, when the hand needs to change position, instead of immediate movement, a laboriously 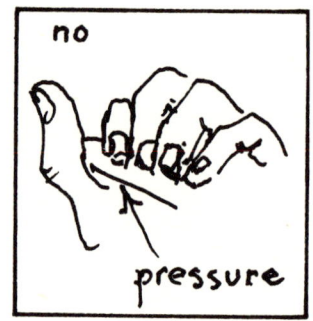 slow ungluing has first to take place in the fingers. When functioning correctly, the thumb should be able to be released quickly and lightly from the neck of the violin at will, for from this comes agility in the fingers and a firm left-hand technique.

Gripping by the thumb also causes it to separate from the unit of the whole hand, so that its true function is lost and it is no longer able to cushion the impact of the fingers. Thus the thumb should move cleanly with the hand in all shifts. Now the part of the thumb best suited to acting as a cushion is naturally the softest part in the upper section, as indi-

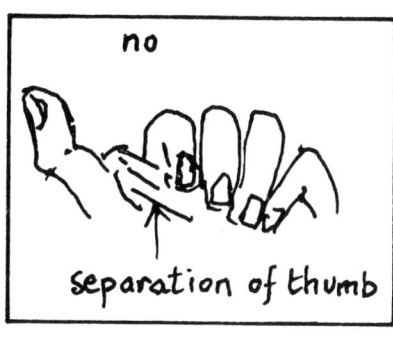

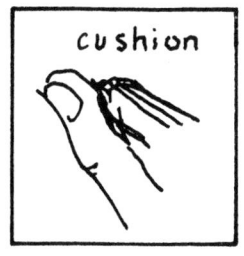

cated in the diagram, and when this position is adopted, the tip of the thumb may be seen projecting a little above the fingerboard. As far as possible this position should be maintained whatever the string or position.

With this guiding concept we can look at some major errors that arise in the hold of the instrument. Often to facilitate moving to the A and E strings, the hand is made to bend at the wrist under the neck of the instrument in the interests of what is considered to be security. (See diagram A.) To counter this, the fingers should retain the position they naturally adopt on the G and D strings, and, with the

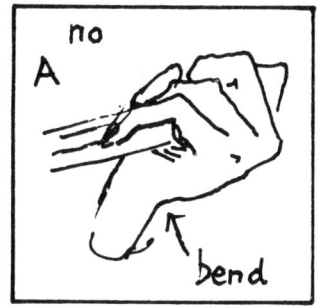

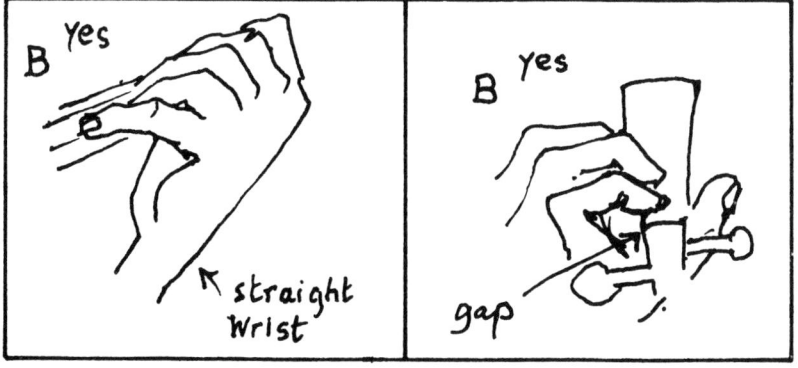

neck still cushioned on the flesh of the thumb, move slightly out from the neck of the instrument, maintaining a straight wrist. (See both diagrams B.) Such a gap, however small, avoids the danger of the hand 'holding' in the wrong sense, and still allows the downwards pressure of the finger to be lightly counterbalanced by the thumb. Nowhere is the need for this counterbalance more clearly seen than in the mechanics of vibrato. If there is any element of control by gripping, the roll on the finger-end (basically giving a forearm movement if there is no bending at the wrist) is severely inhibited: movement is limited to the hand and results in a hard insistency of vibration which denies sensitivity of feeling.

All this, of course, is more readily seen in the lower positions. In the higher positions the thumb is obliged to move wholly under 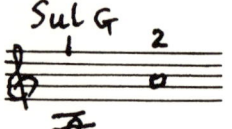 the neck of the violin—say in a shift from the A to the octave A as in the example. But even here its function is to offer a resistant cushion for the downwards force of the fingers. The danger in such a shift is that the hand will bend outwards at the wrist (diagram C), giving an awkward tension in the wrist and the thumb itself. The feeling enjoyed in the first position should be retained as high up the fingerboard as possible; and above all, it should be possible to release the hold of the hand on the neck of the violin at a moment's notice.

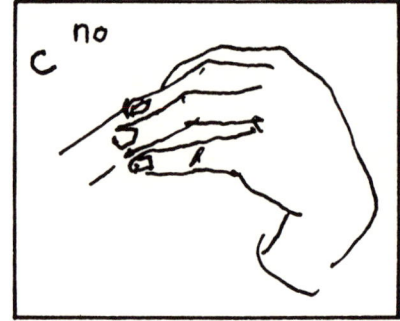

An awareness of the true function of the thumb should be one of the first things to be imparted to a young student, for its abuse has a lasting damaging effect on the left hand. And even more important, before that, a student should be trained to hold the violin between the chin and the shoulder without any aid from the left hand at all. If we do not start from this fundamental point, the left arm and the thumb will surely operate in the wrong way ever afterwards.

11

CO-ORDINATION OF LEFT AND RIGHT

CO-ORDINATION IS, of course, one of the most important factors in the art of playing the violin. Most activities undertaken by man demand co-ordination between his left and right sides, but none more than the playing of a stringed instrument. It is an elementary proposition: in the beginning a student is taught the art of sustaining tone through the bow, and he is also taught mechanical precision in the fingers of the left hand. All that is needed then is co-ordination. But later on when we come to inspect this co-ordination we find that added problems such as dynamics, crossing of strings, and bow control have all added up to interfere with the even flow of power in the right arm. Above all, we find that the actual rhythmic pattern is instigating a corresponding movement in the bow arm causing unevenness in the line of sound.

This state of affairs is related to the inherent symbolism of right and left in the body. The left embodies all that is rational, all that is connected with the physical world, as opposed to the right which symbolises all that is willed: thus the function of the fingers of the left hand is primarily to shape sound patterns where that of the bow is to supply power. In life it is the head that interferes with the will of man, often to the point of paralysis, so that he is unable to make a clear move or decision: the head wants to do one thing and the will another. In fact we have here the primary division in man.

And this is the division in the violin too. The conflict between head and will, between fingers and bow, is still unresolved in quite advanced students. In a passage like the following from the Sonata No. 7 by Mozart, because of confusion between the two sides, the

Co-ordination of Left and Right

two A's are pulled down the bow with a jerk. This faster movement causes an increased dynamic and the A's are too loud and out of context. The normal way of correcting this error is an arbitrary struggle involving endless repetition, but this is ineffectual and only serves to damage the accuracy of the rhythm too. Something has to be done in the interests of synchronisation.

The first stage must be to undo the confusion that exists between the two sides (confusion, *con-fuse*, is what results when parts are wrongly fused together) and to do this, we first have to separate the right arm so that it is independent of the left hand. Let us assume for the exercise that the fingers of the left hand are rhythmically accurate: then we simply eliminate notes, leaving a basic bow pattern played on one note only. For instance, example A can be simplified to example B, and by repeating this simplified version six times or so, a mechanical pattern is established in the right arm. If the rhythmic pattern of the fingers is then reinserted, their interference upon the bow will be found to have lessened considerably.

Of course the left hand may not itself be rhythmically perfect, and work may be needed to clarify rhythms as in examples (d) and (e) that follow. We are suggesting, however, that the sustained evenness of the bow is disturbed in quite simple passages, and it may be necessary to return to lessons of the first violin tutor in order to develop a bow-arm capable of being unruffled by the complexities of the left hand.

In the following examples we must first establish the simplified bow patterns with breadth and assurance before inserting the actual notes. The first three examples are from the same sonata, No. 7 in F by Mozart; example (d) is from the finale of the Sonatina in G minor by Schubert: and (e) is from the Sonata No. 10 in B♭ by Mozart.

(a)

(b)

(c)

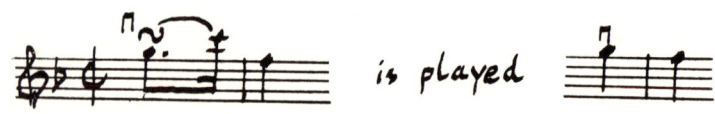

(d)

(e)

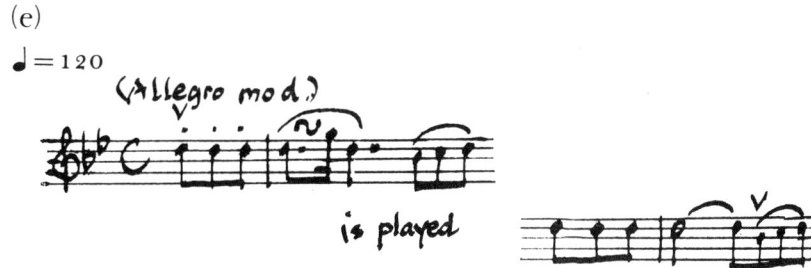

Co-ordination between right and left also suffers in quite a different way. When feeling is intensified by vibrato at the head of a phrase as with the indicated quaver E in the second bar of the example below, there is a tendency for this to be registered in the bow arm too. The bow gathers speed, the dynamic is therefore increased and the sensitivity in that moment is coarsened. In the example, from the opening of the slow movement of the Mozart Violin Concerto in G major, true intensity at the indicated places

comes from the combination of immediately alive vibrato with a perfectly controlled and sustained bow. Emotional impact comes from the *left* hand, not from cumbersome effort from the right arm, and our intensity has seeped away if, at the end of that high E, we find ourselves three-quarters of the way down the bow. Even

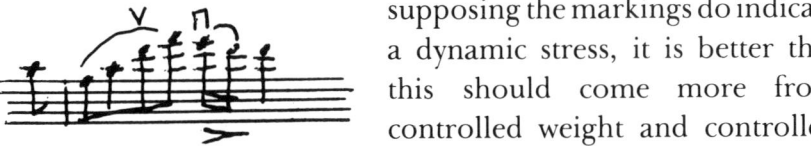

supposing the markings do indicate a dynamic stress, it is better that this should come more from controlled weight and controlled speed at the beginning of the bow rather than from a quick pull down it. There is the same tendency to pull down the bow at the places indicated in these examples from the same movement.

In our three examples, and in all similar instances, the key words are *conservation* in the right and *intensity* in the left.

Conservation and intensity are in a sense opposites, and it is for this reason that it is difficult to co-ordinate them. Like rhythm and the bow, they need to be mastered separately. Thus our example from the Mozart Concerto should be played first purely mechanically without a suggestion of vibrato, so as to establish a simple pattern in the bow-arm. On the other side, a clear concept of where and how vibrato is to be used in relation to the shape of the phrase, is needed. A fusion of the two sides gives controlled intensity, the most powerful of all combinations in music. It is a strange fact, and one that reduces the sense of contradiction, that intensity does not mean rushing or urging, but a holding in, a containing of energy. The Latin word *tenere*, 'to hold', clearly tells us this.

In this exercise we are asked to eliminate any suggestion of vibrato and any extraneous movement from the left fingers, and this in itself is a problem for some. Often, the habit of moving the fingers about edgily as soon as they touch the string, under the name of intensifying feeling, is so strongly ingrained that to try to do without it is virtually impossible. Only by clear understanding of the arbitrariness of this so-called intensity, by studying the mechanics of pure vibrato, and by continual attention, can such a habit be changed.

And finally in the act of playing, there is the most obvious aspect of co-ordination, the co-inciding of the finger as it falls on to the string with the exact point in the change of the bow. This concerns the precision, the strength, and the speed of the fingers as they hit and are released from the string, and these depend very much

Co-ordination of Left and Right

upon the freedom at the knuckle joint whence the action derives. The only remedy for such a difficulty is to observe all actions in slow motion, eliminating anticipation in the fall of the fingers or conversely controlling the bow so that it does not change direction late or early. The factor which fuses both together in this sort of

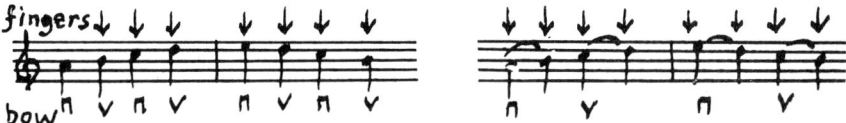

exercise is an absolutely metronomical rhythm, and however simple the actual notes, this rhythmic framework should be maintained.

Some of the more subtle aspects of the co-ordination of the two sides, and the function of right and left have been discussed in *The Simplicity of Playing the Violin*, in the chapter 'Bow and Violin as Male and Female'. In this sense of co-ordination we are talking of a relationship in which the violin yields sensitively under the will of the bow, a process which has considerable similarity to the human male-female situation. Thus, not only is power demanded of the bow-arm, but sensitivity as well: nor must we forget the sense of friction between the bow and string which gives unity to the relationship. A stringed instrument is a unique phenomenon—a thing to be marvelled at. When its two sides become one in the act of playing, we not only have a marriage of passive and active but of ordered design and controlled power. These and many other factors make the violin and the bow, viewed together, the most mysterious and satisfying of instruments the world has ever seen.

12

BODY PARTICIPATION

MANY VIOLINISTS give the impression that their bodies are disassociated from their instruments and from the music they are playing. This is a pity, because the body has an immediate and natural response to music: when we hear music our hands, feet and our whole organism become deeply involved. Again we have to point to the loss of vitality and to a general misuse of the body.

The chief response is, of course, a rhythmic one: a repeated pulse as in the heart-beat, the breathing or in the cyclic rhythm of the cosmos lies at the root of our existence. But not only does the body respond rhythmically to the music, it also wants to make appropriate gestures, to move in a direction and manner that corresponds with the shape and character of the music. Unfortunately, when we learn to play an instrument, especially a stringed instrument, the misuse of the body combines with the complexities of technique and interferes with our natural movements; the wisdom of the body is smothered, and we become over-concerned with unnatural aspects of control and co-ordination between the two sides. But ultimately the playing of music should have the same rhythmic involvement as when we dance. We should feel to be dancing our music.

This does not mean we have to dance about excessively whilst playing; we are talking more of developing an *inner* feeling for the correct gesture; and this entails work against habitual gestures that have accrued from struggling to overcome technical difficulties. If we take a simple up-beat as in the Mozart G major Sonata (marked +), there is often a tendency for the violin at that point to move to the left, to accompany the direction of the bow.

But it is clear that the proper stress is on the first beat of the bar (x), and that any movement in the body belongs here. If we have to describe such a movement, we would say that the violin is still for the up-beat, and leads through a sense of preparation to a yield

under the bow on the down-beat. Certainly the appropriate move is not a swing to the left. Such a gesture as the yield under the bow is of great sensitivity, resembling the uncurling of the petals of a flower to the sun—it is essentially a response to a life force.

Again in the same example, in the context of the whole phrase, the minim G's should be perfectly equal and even, but on the last one there is a suggestion of an opening out to the subsequent down beat (x). In fact this could be written more finely, by adding a long line indicating no change in dynamic or feeling intensity, thus:

It follows that the counterpart to the evenness of these minims is stillness of both body and instrument, so as to allow the preparation for the yield of the violin under the bow on the F♯ minim down-beat. A general rule about this could be given: where tone is to be even, the body remains still, and where the music has significant shape, a corresponding gesture should be sensed. On the other hand, the situation can be reversed, for a still body tends to encourage an even tone, and a naturally felt gesture tends to determine the shape of the music. Apart from pure mechanics, these are the only type of movements valid whilst playing; and they are important because they reinforce the music instead of going against it. They are at the same time functional and beautiful.

There are parallel situations throughout music. Here is another example, from the Schubert A minor Sonatina:

The eight semiquavers require perfect stillness in the body, and the only useful movement affirms the head of the phrase on the crotchet E (marked with a ×).

It should be clear from what has been said that the movement referred to is more in the nature of a relationship between bow and instrument, with the violin yielding to the authority of the bow. In this sense, we are again in the field of the dance, because a dance, on one level, is a ceremonial play between male and female. This aspect of the bow as male and the violin as female has been discussed at some length in *The Simplicity of Playing the Violin*. The relationship between bow and violin is in fact like a ceremonial dance, because in a true technique are to be found all the constituent parts of the dance. There are all shades of relationship as in the dance and they include a sensitive yield, a harmonious and mutual balance of power and violent aggression. These and many more can be found in our original example:

At the two places marked (×), we find the sensitive yield just described. At (+), the bow rests on the string, poised, like the dragon-fly hovering before its next dart forward; or, in terms of the dance, like the still poise where the female yield and the male thrust are held in equi-balance. At (□), the bow aggressively bites into the string, an expression of the male dominance in the dance. But on a purely mechanical level in such gestures between bow and violin, it has to be understood that the movement is a vertical one as in the everyday gesture of bowing from the waist. This is the true yield: to alter the angle of the instrument or to shift it to the side evasively does not contribute to the music. We are asking for participation from the body, not interference from unrelated movement.

We cannot talk of *dancing* music without involving the feet. In the chapter on 'The inertia of the body', we spoke of the sole of the foot taking the balance of the body; and when we consider the relationship between gesture and music, we cannot help but see that if music is a dance at all, the *whole* body is involved, including the feet. In a passage like the following in the Allegretto from the

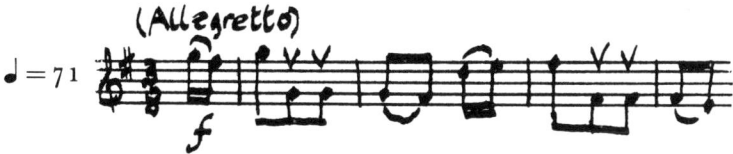

same Mozart Sonata, there is a natural play in the feet and a slight shift of stress from one foot to the other. Moreover we can see generally as we play that there is a recurrent pattern in the way this stress is taken in the body: when we affirm in the music, the weight of the body shifts on to the left foot. In the Handel Sonata No. 5 in A major:

two such places are indicated. Affirmation of the stress in the music could never be effected by moving on to the right foot. This principle operates everywhere in life where right and left are concerned. When, for instance, the right arm is raised to deliver a blow, it is the left leg that counter-balances the downwards force. The reader is invited to play the Handel example just quoted, taking the weight on the right foot at the indicated cross, to feel how totally out of correspondence with the music such a gesture is. But again we are not dealing in measurable rules: having understood the general principle, exaggeration should be avoided; such feeling is more inwardly experienced than externalised. Nevertheless there *is* life in the feet; there is a yield at the waist; there is a different function in the two sides of the body; and all are related to the music.

This is the reason why the sitting position, the lot of most violinists, is essentially unsatisfactory. The feet and legs, the most immediate expressors of rhythm are out of use, and movement is only possible from the waist upwards. If this example from the same Mozart sonata is played standing, we feel vital throughout the body—and the vitality starts, so to speak, from the feet:

Also, as part of the whole movement, at the up-bow quavers indicated, the violin is lifted upwards with spirit. (The violin does not however separate from the body.) In the sitting position, with the movement confined to the upper part of the body, a real challenge presents itself to players in orchestras and quartets, for then the vitality stems from a flexible waist.

It is surprising, in observing an average student, to see how many of these gestures are completely at variance with what the music demands. This comes from a generally incorrect use of the body and from the struggle to overcome technical difficulties. Such a misuse of the body can be seen during an expanding phrase, when the violin can often be seen being lowered. Clearly, not only is it logical for the violin to be raised along with the expanding music, but expansion in itself is a positive force psychologically. In the theme from the Mozart Sonata in G major, it would be out of

correspondence to lower the violin at the end of the second bar (x), because at this place a build is demanded towards the first beat of the subsequent bar. In the Courante of the Bach Suite for Cello transcribed for viola, there would similarly be no

correspondence with the music if the instrument were to be lowered during the semiquavers leading into the next bar.

In principle, then, the rule is that physical expansion goes with musical expansion, always bearing in mind that we are dealing with shades of feeling almost too intangible for expression through words. If we wish, however, we can see the logic of the correspondence in caricature. If we play the semiquavers of the

foregoing example at a slower speed, and as we do so take a slow inbreath and slightly raise the instrument, then on the minim B release the breath and gently lower the violin, we feel the process has been whole and perfectly natural. If on the other hand, we now play the semiquavers, this time breathing out and lowering the instrument, there is a sense of conflict—the body and the music become almost totally immobilised. Such a conflict is no different to shaking the head whilst saying 'Yes'; the body rebels when it is directed to do something out of correspondence with a feeling it naturally endorses. The exercise is, of course, only to demonstrate a principle, and breathing especially is not to be taken too literally; a violinist beathes ultimately with his bow. Nevertheless the body gives wing to the music, and without a correspondence between it and the music, playing is greatly impoverished. What should be understood is that the body intuitively knows that correspondence: it has its own wisdom.

We have yet to mention another aspect of the body's participation in the playing of music, and this can best be described as a preparation for an entry or an attack. Any violent physical act involves the mobilisation of energy. We do not hit a nail with a hammer without first raising the hammer and poising it above the level of the object to be hit; a swimmer does not dive into the water without mobilising energy in the bent knees and keyed feet, for it is from here that he unleashes his spring to action. In both instances there is a compacting of potential energy in that position of preparation. We see the same function in the conductor's up-beat: besides setting a tempo it prepares an entry through inducing a state of tension in the player without which there is no attack. The effect of non-preparation is equivalent to firing a catapult with an insufficiently taut elastic. But we clearly do not screw up the physical muscles into a contracted state or our movement would be impeded. What happens is that we first draw in our energy on a subtle level, our intention to act tightens the field forces permeating our organism, and that is embodied in the appropriate gesture.

For the violinist, the visible part of the mobilised energy is a slight raising of the violin and bow (felt as one unit), which acts, like the conductor, as a preparatory up-beat; and this is followed by a quick release back to the original position upon the attack itself. Such a preparation is indispensable, for instance, at the beginning of the Bach Double Concerto, where the cross in the

example marks a felt preparation a crotchet in value: or in the Scherzo of Beethoven's Fourth Symphony, where the cross indicates a preparation on the second beat of the empty bar, the

value of a dotted crotchet. But music is full of such examples, and whatever the dynamics or tempo, even when we cannot accurately refer to an 'attack', there is always an intuitively felt preparation in the body. Such points of preparation are important to us as players, for without them we lose our own vitality and the interest of an audience.

These are just some of the ways in which the body participates during the playing of music. It may be thought by some unnecessary to have analysed them in such detail, but the fact is that the body today exists at such a poor level of efficiency that what was once a natural endowment has now to be recovered by painstaking training. It has become hard, and with that, our work of recovery has become commensurately hard. Natural power has been dammed up and the flow has to be released. When we *damn* a person in the sense of a curse, we will to keep that flow of divine energy trapped inside him so that he remains in a condition of error. To some degree a man is able to release that energy through dancing, but the complexities of technique on a stringed instrument are enormous, and he has to work very hard in this field. Few would doubt that the best players *look* as though their instruments are part of their bodies and that the music appears to dance through them.

13

THE DANGER OF MUSIC STANDS AND MUSIC

IF THERE is one certain pitfall in the early stages of learning the violin, it is the combined effect of leaning downwards to read music from a low stand and fixing the eyes rigidly upon the music. It may seem too elementary an issue for consideration, but the cumulative effect over the years is to make an unyielding body, unable to respond to the shape of the music in the way we have discussed in the previous chapter, and to establish a wrong posture of the body and angle of the instrument.

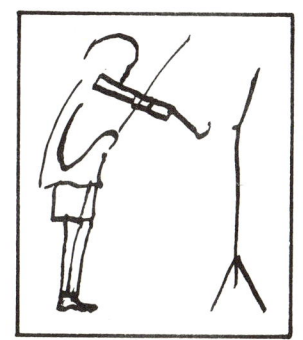

In *The Simplicity of Playing the Violin* the most efficient angle was given as about 20° off level and falling just slightly under parallel to the ground, giving seen head on, and seen from the side. Such angles, we saw, give a healthy relationship between right and left sides in which the bow is able to assume a position of command over the instrument. Now music played on the stand, as in the diagram above, is lower than eye level, so that the violin is actually in the line of vision. For the music to be completely open to view, the violin has to be moved to the left of the music or underneath it. Both these corrective movements have

unhappy consequences. Movement to the left separates the violin from the whole unit of the body so that the arm has difficulty in moving the bow at a constant 90° to the string, and to drop the violin downwards hunches up the body and denies freedom of style and a firm contact between bow and string. The only remedy is to heighten the music, if anything to slightly above eye level (though care has to be taken not to over-raise the level of the violin). This simple move is often the first stage  in bringing the violin to a more central position and correcting a forward and downward position caused through repeated use of a low stand.

Not only has the posture suffered simply from badly placed music, but there is a very strong tendency to lean forward through the effort to get to grips with difficulties in the music, to fix the attention on it through anxiety. This, as we have said, makes for a rigid body which does not respond to the needs of the music. In fact, the fixing of eyes on the music is an enemy of music-making in every way. If the eyes are allowed to follow the edge of a page, it will be seen that they move in a series of jerks, and that in reading one line of this book, for instance, there will be perhaps five or six stopping places for the eyes. There is in fact no *continuous* flow of vision. Thus, gripping on to something with the eyes in anxiety only exaggerates the very mechanics of seeing, and sums up every aspect of the arch-enemy, contraction, that has been studied in this book. It is fairly obvious from this that in playing from music, the comprehension of a whole phrase will be inhibited if only a little of it is seen at a time. This is why reading from a written page is essentially against the spirit of music; music is a whole experience from the heart, but one disjointed by broken vision.

To safeguard against the dangers of the stoop forward and over-fixing by the eyes, first we must see to the height of the stand, and second the eyes have to learn to move lightly from point to point in a way that we can best describe as skimming over the music. Fixation must be avoided at all costs; it hardens both the muscles of the eyes and inhibits the freedom of the whole body and the spirit of the music. Third, if at all possible, the written page should be discarded and the music committed to memory. Only then will music be realised internally and the musician play directly from his imagination. Written notation, like everything else in this complex age, is a literal fact which tends to cover up live reality, and in the end is only a vehicle that has to be discarded to move into a new dimension.

14

MECHANICS DETERMINE MUSIC

As there is a danger in identification with the written notation, so too there is a danger that too much concentration upon mechanical issues destroys the spirit of the music and the sheer pleasure in playing. Certainly most students have to face this conflict at some time in their lives, when they feel that work on mechanical details is draining away all interest in their instrument. And yet imagination without a logical technical structure gives arbitrary and unfinished results. It is the art of successful teaching to steer a delicate course between technical work and creative imagination, so that in the end they are unified. Whatever sphere we look at, whether it be one of the arts or physical activity, that dilemma is found; and it is also in the problem of the young today, who, living in a prevalent spirit against fastidious work, tend to denigrate its importance. Work *is* necessary to allow the birth of imagination. And where ultimately a fusion of scientific analysis and art is achieved, we are conscious neither of the laboriousness of analysis nor of the lack of restraint in the imagination. Greatness comes of such a fusion: a great scientist is one who has fired his theory by imagination, and a great artist is one who has restrained riotous imagination by the clarity of technique.

How does the violinist stand in relation to this problem? His aim, as we have said, is to transcend mechanics so as to break through into a world of creative imagination. In common sense terms, a student has to realise that any and every mechanical action he makes has its exact counterpart in sound. A very obvious statement, it may be said. But is it? Most teachers will have experienced the difficulty of convincing a student anxious to keep up with his fellows, that only a close study of mechanics will correct his errors—that his enthusiastic playing of difficult works will get him nowhere. He does not want to see that every over-pressed down-bow interfering with the flow of sound, every up-bow slowing down the tempo at the heel through contraction, every interference in the right arm from the rhythmic pattern in the left hand, every malfunction caused through wrong stance—all these and many more factors *determine the sound he produces*. Let two short examples from the Handel Sonata in E major demonstrate this point:

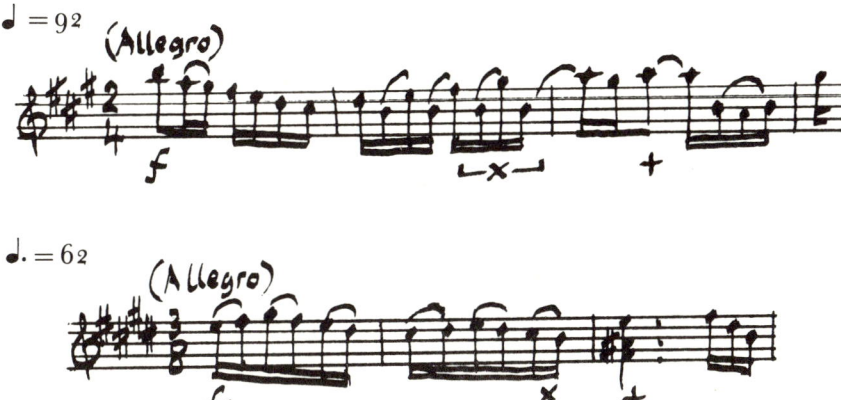

In each example it is a mistake for the first two bars to be played in the upper half of the bow, for the bow is then wrongly situated in the third bar (indicated +). In the first the tied A, and in the other the dotted quaver chord, do not have the necessary length of bow, and the sound is strangulated. Clearly there has to be an intention to move towards the heel during the second bar, with a preparatory broadening on the notes marked (x). This is a simple question of mechanics, which we have agreed can be tedious.

So we have to counter this danger, as we have said, by working from both ends of the stick. Dry mechanics have now to give way to the sense of the music. Having studied a particular mechanical issue, a student must now *imagine* the shape of a whole phrase and let it come to life from within him without any other consideration. It does not matter at this point that the mechanics may let him down—the main thing is that the *music* should speak. Using the two Handel excerpts again, we will observe, if we have truly let the music speak, that there is a feeling of it cutting through technical blocks, that it is actually moving the bow towards the right place for it. We are now at the other end of the pole and it seems as if the spirit of the music is actually willing to clarify the mechanics for us. It is true that problems will not immediately be dispelled, but the positive effect of this approach is undeniable. Not only does it appear, as we have said, to penetrate a particular mechanical problem, but it serves to reveal other weaknesses which suddenly, it seems, stand in the way of the perfect form of the music. For instance, in this example from the Lalo Symphonie Espagnole:

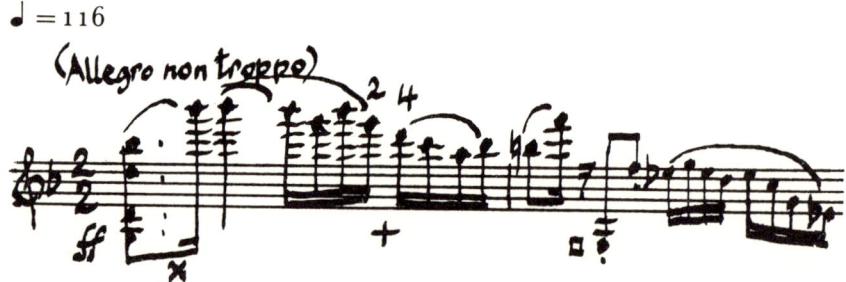

an attempt to let the music speak for itself may reveal such errors as: (a) the leap to the top B♭ being anticipated (×); (b) the shift down from the 2nd to the 4th finger being audible through lack of agility (+); (c) the jump over to the G string being late (□)—all three through states of tension inhibiting the flow of the music. We may then take these revealed weaknesses and work upon them.

The aim of moving between these two poles, work on mechanics and development of imagination, is to fuse them together. There is a similar process in human existence. Shortcomings we know to be within ourselves, and with which we are trying to come to terms, can depress us by their apparent immovability: at times we can only see error and the need for more work. And yet we also know there is potentially a perfect state in ourselves, a higher state which is the right and prerogative of all human beings. It cannot be said to be our property, but we can act *in faith* as though it were. Error holds it back, as poor technique holds back true phrasing. But its power inherently is to penetrate back into the darkness of error, as the free flow of the music does with our technical problems.

A true fusion where mechanics and imagination are equally balanced is rare, but work towards this end will ultimately bear fruit. A teacher's role is to show the relationship between a mechanical action and the sound that action is responsible for; it is only when a student has seen that relationship for himself that he will work with conviction. But equally the teacher's role is to show that a vision of the whole music can help to reveal and dispel those mechanical issues. The point of fusion is where art begins.

15

THE POWER OF IMAGERY

THE QUESTION of imagery follows naturally from the previous chapter. In opening ourselves to the spirit of the music how are we sure we have the perfectly shaped phrase which we have suggested can cut through dry problems of mechanics? Who knows when he has found it?

Individuals work from many different levels, it is true, and many appear to have gifts that others do not have, so that we call some men geniuses, and some natural musicians, whilst others seem incapable of having an immediate comprehension of the shape of music. Despite this, players can be freed from many of the inertias of the body and from erroneous attitudes that have kept them from such an intuitive comprehension. So committed have men become to the literal word, and so externalised by the senses, that real rhythmic precision, understanding of phrase shape and sense of pitch have seriously atrophied. But these faculties are there, buried underneath long-worn habits—they are the birthright of all men; for a *habit*, as the word indicates, is only a garment that has been put on consistently until its owner is no longer aware he wears it.

A student who has difficulty in playing a phrase with a true feeling for its shape, will more likely than not produce a more musical result if he is asked to sing that phrase. The reason is that singing, like dancing, is a more natural mode of expression— breathing has a naturally phasic activity which relates to the phrase in music, and it is this the bow has with difficulty to recover in face of its technical problems. But, a singing teacher would also say that the same errors we have been discussing also interfere with his student's rendering—that he too has not understood the true shape of the music.

This leads us to one stage further back to the only other possible level, to inner experience. We have said that a violinist may benefit from singing the melody he is about to play, but if that melody has not first been experienced or heard *internally*, he will not express it correctly either through his voice or his instrument. The title of this chapter is 'The Power of Imagery'. Anything created has first to be imagined—it is first an inner experience: a cup has first of all to be in the potter's mind's eye before his hand shapes the clay; a cathedral was envisaged by the mason before it rose to the skies in stone; a wood-carver sees his end form before he begins to work, or he would never have the courage to use his chisel; a piece of music is heard by the composer before it is committed to paper. Certainly a player has to recover what the composer imagined before his instrument can transmit it as sound. The same works on a more general level in life: what is imagined strongly enough can be achieved, and the more intense the imagining of the desired result, the quicker and more complete will be that result. In this sense, *imagination* is the root of *magic* in its connotation of the mystery of the magician.

And why, it may be asked, should that internal image be any more desirable than the externalised attempt we are holding to question? We repeat, it is because deep down inside all men is the memory and knowledge of a perfect formal relationship of notes we call phrasing, as well as a pin-head awareness of rhythm and a pure sense of pitch; and if this is so, all that has to be done is to abandon the many interferences that now stand in the way. Of these, surely the written note is the first that should be discarded. To memorise a passage means to eliminate thought and allow the birth of imagination; to memorise and then *let the music come to life* internally is the way to the hidden springs. This pure musical well is like the well of the pure spirit—it is there and only needs re-tapping.

What has to be developed, then, is inner hearing as opposed to outer hearing. Take as an example the opening of the Allegro from the Bach A major Sonata: the build of the phrase through to

the high A must be first heard inwardly, not necessarily in terms of dynamics but in terms of feeling and direction—and then similarly with the descent in the second bar. That image should then be transferred immediately into act, remembering that *immediate* has the very precise meaning of 'without meditation'.

The imagining process is the ground of magic in playing, in the sense of the spell over an audience. In this sense music has the same element of mystery as the magic of the magician. It is the most powerful element in life. The root *mag* means 'great', and this is made clear in the symbolism of the Tarot cards, where the Magician is the Creator of the Universe.

Or take the second theme from the Mozart Rondo in G major: there is a natural movement to the crochet G at the beginning of

the second bar. The aim is obviously to throw away individual beats and to hear the whole shape internally; then to try to produce the magic.

It may be that the student has to learn something of the finished result by emulation of a teacher; it may be that this will help to draw out his ability to recognise truth in music. But the aim in teaching is to foster the capacity for imagination from the student's own inner resources. In this sense, the process is, like that of true education, a leading out of *what is already there*. The creator is there in everyone, waiting to be brought to life.

16

THE MYSTERY OF RHYTHM

WHATEVER ASPECT of music we consider, we are faced with the need to release unnecessary tensions. Tension we must have, but of the right sort. The same can be said of attention, the only difference between the two being that attention is a mental rather than a physical process. (Attention in relation to study has been discussed at length in *The Simplicity of Playing the Violin*).

The idea behind attention is in the *ten* part of the word. The meaning is from the Latin *tenere* 'to hold', suggesting that something is held in or contained. If we do something with attention it means that we focus our minds and do not allow other images, memories or thoughts to interfere. But there is a positive and a negative side to this, as to all things: if our minds hold something in a relentless grip—the same grip we have observed in the physical body—then we have a *tension*, a tightening or holding in, in a destructive sense. Such mental tension does not achieve its objective: it results at its worst in physical pains and in certain circumstances assumes such proportions as to cause a man's complete breakdown.

The attention we are seeking in its positive aspect, then, is more to do with *awareness*. Awareness basically means 'being awake' and carries with it a suggestion of lightness and mobility. If we are truly awake during the whole time we study, we will accomplish any aim we may set ourselves. But to keep awake in this way is difficult because man's supreme gifts, his reason and his consciousness of individual identity, take him away from immediate awareness and put in its place a trap of duality inherent in time. He spends his time weighing up past experience in order to determine future action, and is scarcely ever still and aware in the present moment of time.

Now rhythm is clearly concerned with tension, tension epitomised by the skin of the drum through which it is expressed. It goes without saying that rhythm is not an activity of the mind—it is a very deep awareness within a man, implanted in his physical substance, a living part of the force which animates and sustains the whole universe. Its essential characteristic is that it imposes some sort of order on to what would otherwise be a chaotic sea of energy, and everything that exists can be seen to be beating out its own particular frequency and rhythmic pattern of behaviour. A man's heart-beat and his breathing are both such rhythmic processes internal to him, whilst other rhythms operate outside him everywhere in the cosmos. This does not mean, however, that the universe is run on completely predictable lines. The mechanical patterns may give way to an inner flux, so that in the rhythm of the seasons, for example, there is a quickening movement of growth at the beginning of summer, or in the rhythm of waves in the sea there is variable movement within regular patterns. In music, the Romantic period is full of such variability. In the opening of the Schumann Violin Sonata in A minor, for example:

we feel the urging forward through to the head of the phrase so that the bar-lines are not strictly metronomically accurate, and yet we can still be playing rhythmically. We are referring more to a sense of flow. In fact the Greek root of our word 'rhythm' means 'to flow', so pointing to the fact that though we are giving a regular pulse we are also concerned with giving a sense of continuity to the music. Thus rhythm is both the pulse and the life itself, and there is no wonder that it underlies the whole process of breathing and phrasing. We may be sure that whether it be Schumann, Bach or the most simple four-square folk tune, the success of a performance depends upon 'flow'.

But a sense of rhythm seems to present immense problems to students; this controlled flow is the hardest thing to achieve. Why is this so? The answer is: Because it is not possible to achieve a free flow without a prior ability to play rhythmically in the strictly metrical sense. And here is where we have to turn back to the idea of 'attention', for attention is very much a part of the self-awareness that is now peculiar to man. Initially he experienced rhythms within and outside him on an intuitive level, and gradually, as awareness of self increased, and as he saw himself more in relation to the world, he began to exploit his powers, of which rhythm was one, to satisfy a creative need. But such a self-awareness was achieved only at the expense of egotism and an over-grown intellect, and in this sense, Western man died to intuition. It is only in the East, and especially in the dances of primitive tribes, that an extraordinary sensitivity to rhythm has been retained, because these peoples have not yet reached this point; their consciousness is not yet individually orientated. It is the hair-splitting analysing of the cerebral civilisations that has finally usurped that power.

What we are saying is that civilisation has brought a wealth of complexity, an overgrowth of analysis, seen in music as harmonic laws, relationship of keys, pitch and melody, to which we in this age are accustomed, but that it is just this that has made it more difficult to retain the simple intuitive rhythm awareness which was at one time the prerogative of all men. So that now, somehow, a player has to cut through that overgrowth; he has to discover the finest possible awareness within himself, to put himself on a pin-head where he is constantly awake to the forces in him. He has to live in the moment of *now*. If he does this he is fusing his raw energy with self-awareness. Rhythm is not just a raw repetitive hammering; it is as fine a thing as the mental and formalising forces in the music it animates. It is fundamentally a tension—a holding in of energy.

A teacher may use the expression 'hold it' to a student whose rhythm is rushing away out of control. And for a few moments his awareness may return, but then more often than not it lapses. He has to be reminded and reminded again, to be brought back to a state of awareness. Often during orchestral concerts the whole of a section, it seems, runs herd-like out of control; its members have lost that awareness of the precipice they should be treading. *Anticipation*—the word means 'experiencing in advance'—kills a performance: and this can only happen if awareness has been lost. On yet another count, therefore, it is necessary to turn back inside from outer to inner experience. The chapters on music stands and on the power of imagery both point to the same thing.

It can be seen from this that the breathing process and the suspense in it, to be discussed in the following chapter, is closely connected with rhythm. The whole time in playing music we have to guard against anticipation, for it signifies either interference from the mind looking ahead, or the leaking of awareness from the now-moment. *Attention* and *tension*—as light as the spider's web yet rivetting the playing to the audience with the same power as a cat's hypnotic transfixing of the bird. This is the essence of rhythm; it is what joins dead black notes, as these from the *Eine*

kleine Nachtmusik, into a continuous flow. (The crucial points are marked with an arrow.) Only when we have this control can we successfully move into the more subtle fields of rhythm where the razor-edge metre gives way to and is incorporated in a bigger flow which links all possible points into one whole.

17

THE BREATH OF LIFE

MUCH HAS been said about breathing in the author's previous books. The field is inexhaustible. A breath is one filling and emptying of the lungs and resembles all phasic processes, whether it be a cycle of the seasons, one complete day, or the rise and fall of a civilisation, in having a high point of maturity followed by a gradual descent into darkness. In all these instances there is a crucial point in that darkness, a point of uncertainty. In the seasons it is the point just after the winter solstice when it is not yet certain whether the sun will rise again. (When in fact it does so appreciably two days after the solstice, the birth of Christ is celebrated.) In the day, it is the moment of deepest darkness when it is not certain that the light will overpower the dark (each sunrise is in this sense a birth and a triumph). And in the cycle of civilisations, it is the point where all appears to be chaos; the lowest ebb has been reached and there is doubt as to the possibility of any future order. (Here again, life has been stirring imperceptibly, and as with the medieval cathedrals after the Dark Ages, there is a sudden re-birth into light.) In each case, a new breath has been taken and life goes on.

But there is always the point of crisis, the point of doubt. Is the light going to return? Making music has a close affinity with breathing and depends upon this point of doubt for transmitting a heightened awareness to the listener. *Is* life going to continue? We are held in suspense. It is what keeps life interesting, the unpredictability of it. That is why the poise at the end of a phrase is one of the most important tools at the performer's disposal. If we take away that space between two phrases we take away the element of doubt, and with it the interest of the audience. It is a strange thing that music should exist on the basis of doubt, but it is so.

Thus a violinist has to study and value the moment of doubt, the suspense before the birth of a new phrase. In this excerpt from the Mozart Concerto in D major:

♩ = 120

the music depends upon his manipulation of the poise between phrases, indicated here by the lines. The phrase beginnings have almost to be delayed to affirm the surprise that life goes on, and a good performance is full of many such deaths of the old and emerging of the new. If, as teacher, we can make a student *breathe* his music, we can replace heaviness and stagnation by suspense and life. These moments of poise in the following example from the same concerto, again hold us on a thread of uncertainty too delicate for definition.

With a longer gap between phrases, the danger of anticipation, and the loss of our element of doubt, is increased manifold. In Mozart's Sonata No. 7 for instance, the places indicated by the

♩ = 125

lines are literally a catching of the breath such as we would experience in a heightened emotional state. One could of course argue that our suspense is measurable in terms of rhythm, that it is simply a question of keeping exact time. But under analysis this is clearly not the case. Our lungs and hearts work rhythmically, but sensitivity of feeling is something beyond that, something unpredictable. Rhythm and feeling both tread on a precipice-edge, but feeling is the human element that redeems the machine. In the following example from the first movement of the Mozart Sonata in B♭:

a clinically accurate rhythm would only produce boredom in the listener. Interest is kept alive by unwritten moments of suspense at the places indicated by the lines, and in addition by a sense of the whole moving progressively towards the indicated E♭. We can go no  further in music than to tread the precipice of rhythmic precision and combine it with unpredictability and suspense in the breath.

This may seem an elaborate rationalisation of what is a natural process in playing. But it is often the first step towards helping a player to recover his lost sensitivity. After that, his task is to make a live experience of his analysis, to transform cold dots on paper into the breathing of his body. More than that: his task is also to teach the limbs of the physical body to breathe in their own way. The simplest experiment will show that muscular tensions in fingers and arms at the moments of the suspense of the breath, destroy the lightness we are seeking: to grip the bow at these points interferes with the control of the next entry. So that where there is a musical suspense, we should also look for a suspense of effort from the body. At these places in the Mozart sonata already quoted, the bow rests lightly on the string, more in the sense of hovering, without tensions in the fingers or arm. Similarly in re-taken chords (as in the example from the Mozart Sonata No. 7) the bow, having returned to the heel, rests lightly on the string prior to the next attack.

In these and many other instances the body participates in the suspense in the music, and body and soul, so to speak, become one felt whole.

We can now look at a perhaps unexpected aspect of breathing in music. The shape of a whole phrase is often indicated by the curved glyph ⌒ and this would often be better expressed by the glyph ⟨≻ used for dynamics, since it shows the actual head of the phrase. But individual stresses within that whole phrase are always felt as out-breaths; the rhythmic impulse demands that they should be pushed out in the shape of a sigh, thus: ≻— The last movement of the Mozart Concerto in A major

has basically a two-bar phrase-shape. But the music throughout depends on inner sighs that we can now add in the form of hair-pins, and the whole becomes almost an exercise in breathing, very apparent when the passage is sung. Ideally, of course, the

music would be more complete, with the overall phrase, hairpin, and added commas, but at this point, our attempt to commit music to paper begins to assume absurd proportions.

The question of the inner sigh needs constant attention in instrumental playing, especially since, due to faulty mechanics in the bow arm, the sigh tends to be reversed. In the 3rd, 4th and 5th bars of the quotation which follows from Schubert's G minor

Sonatina, the music demands an emphasis at the beginning of each crotchet, which can be intensified by the immediate use of vibrato. But teachers know well the tendency for the shape of the sigh to be reversed and for vibrato to emerge on the second note, giving the following effect:

There is no more common fault in string playing than this, and none more destructive to the shape of music.

Again, in the Mozart Rondo in C major, though nothing is

specified, lines over the two up-bow quavers in each bar obviously indicate breaks. But the sound we need would more accurately be

represented by sighs and commas. If we were asked to define this in mechanical terms we would say that each note is composed of (a) an immediate push from the bow; (b) a release of pressure immediately after the beginning of the note; (c) a suspense at the end of the note which

acts as a preparation for the next. All this can be found in an already-quoted example from the Mozart Sonata in B♭, and again hairpins and commas would more accurately designate the sound we are seeking.

Limitless examples can be used to show how music, if it is to live, must first breathe. But everywhere what we find is faulty mechanics standing in the way. Let us look at a passage from the

Schubert Sonatina in G minor. Normally, on the opening crotchets, we hear either a flat and unyielding sound or there is a bulge after the beginning of the note, giving this effect: whereas the sound we seek is like our previous examples

where the sound is released evenly. The bulge comes from excessive weight in the arm, due to the inability to release the forearm from the upper arm after  the middle of the bow. And conversely on the up-bow, weight arrives too late because of the difficulty of applying weight from the hand at the beginning of the note. Because this is a common error, detached notes need to be studied from the very beginning, releasing weight through the length of the bow with such a feeling of expired breath. (Vibrato, used to emphasise this shape, is discussed in a later appropriate chapter.)

But these important subtleties in music cannot be written in notation; we cannot find these moments of suspense indicated. Quite short notes may need to be broken by points of repose and

the faster they are, the more condensed and difficult is the process. In the Mozart Rondo the music requires repose after each quaver, which in effect means separating all the notes. There are many

similar instances. In the last movement of the Dvořák Sonatina there is an obvious need for a clear break before and after the quavers indicated despite the faster tempo, so that the pattern would be more accurately notated:

And the same applies in the following example from the Mozart Sonata No. 10 in B♭, where the difficulty is in making a convincing break after the second quaver in each bar.

Breath, however it is seen, is a great mystery. When we cease to breathe we cease to live. It is the only one of the four elements, fire, air, water, earth, which lives simultaneously within and without the body. Thus it has a dual function, relating the outer to the inner and the spiritual to the material. Breath sustains life in a most delicate way, again a dual process, for when air is taken in, penetrating the delicate tissues of the lungs, it enters the bloodstream and regenerates the body, giving it life; then the poisons that have accumulated in the tissues are given back to the bloodstream and thence to the lungs to be discharged as carbon monoxide. Here is our duality again, a cycle of life and death.

We have said that breath relates the spirit and the body of man. Now the experiences of the spirit undergone in that body constitute his soul life. This soul life is concerned largely with defence, either of physical life itself or of an egotistic identity, and a man is at the mercy of emotional states stemming from some form of fear connected with that defence. Fear causes the blood to be directed to the organs connected with flight and self-protection, and this in turn causes quicker and more disturbed breathing. Uneven breathing is the indicator of an uneven inner state. But by the same token, even breathing can turn back inwards and through the control of the heart-beat bring about a stiller emotional state. This is why controlled breathing may be used as a mediator, a counter to a diseased modern psyche which is bedevilled by fear, and why in any situation a musician may use it as a general help for a nervous state.

Art too is a mediator between man's spirit and his material existence, and an artist is for ever trying to reconcile the apparently irreconcilables. Thus art is to some extent like breath—it deals with pulls, the flux between life and death. It is concerned with the doubt with which we started the chapter, and it is the reason why breathing lies behind our performances as musicians. Of all the arts, music is the nearest to actual live experience, and can teach a man about his state uniquely, mysteriously, through the way of intuition.

18

SOME ERRORS IN VIBRATO

THE ROOT meaning of vibrato is 'life'; and with good reason. It puts interest into flat sound and makes dead music vibrate with life, a fact which was recognised by all the main early writers on the violin, including Simpson and Rousseau in the seventeenth and Geminiani and Leopold Mozart in the eighteenth centuries. The mechanics of vibrato and the way it determines the quality of the sound have been discussed in the author's first book. It was said that a warm and pleasurable sound depends first upon evenness in the vibratory movement which constitutes vibrato, and that this is made much more difficult with the action limited to the hand or the fingers; also, with the action so limited, it is difficult to achieve any modification in the frequency of the movement. For these and other reasons, a case was presented for the wider vibrato stemming from the use of the forearm.

The restricted movement inherent in a finger or wrist vibrato comes in the first place from every student's problem of holding the instrument. The original insecurity of the violin between chin and shoulder causes the hand to grip the neck of the instrument, and the hand's main concern is then to stop it from falling. Vibrato can only be natural once the instrument can be held securely without help from the hand, and to allow a student to attempt it without this having been established is to spell its death before the attempt begins. Vibrato comes from a *roll* on the finger-end, which, given a secure hold of the instrument, gives rise to a natural movement of the forearm. Having said that, our term 'forearm' vibrato is not entirely accurate since the finger contributes the actual roll, and the upper arm, which one might suppose to be non-active, can be shown to be in considerable motion. Despite this, the total action is essentially a yield at the elbow which gives rise to a movement of the forearm, and the term 'forearm' vibrato is more one of reference, safeguarding from the start the dangers of bending at the wrist and restriction to the fingers.

In trying to achieve this vibrato, then, it is better not to make a conscious effort to move the forearm, but to concentrate on the roll of the finger-end, allowing the yield at the elbow to happen of its own accord. We must remember that much depends on maintaining a straight line from the knuckles and the elbow, and, if this is done, errors caused through 'holding' the instrument in a state of tension can quickly be remedied. Also, it is worth noting that in the end we cannot be over-rigid about adhering to the forearm movement: the fingers may be used and modifications permitted, but only when rules have been thoroughly assimilated.

As for the actual sound, anyone who doubts the different qualities produced by using the fingers, wrist and forearm, should listen consecutively to three players who profess to avail themselves of these different methods. The functions of the different parts of the arm, already referred to, will be found to operate here with a ruthless logic. A finger vibrato produces on the whole a fast and irritable quality of sound, equivalent to the excitable discharge of mental activity, devoid of feeling. Wrist vibrato, though warmer, is still consistently wobbly and un-varying. Both inevitably show the limitations of using a tool not in sympathetic correspondence with the task it is required to carry out. In short, in any field the hand stands for and expresses articulative power, not for feeling or energy. The forearm, pliable and adaptable, unlike the hand or upper arm, is intrinsically to do with expressing feeling, and in life registers emotion through gesture. The upper arm comes into the picture very little, for it is the source of power, and this is in no way connected with the function of vibrato. (It is the right arm where the upper arm is in evidence, for here, as we have seen elsewhere, its role is to affirm power.) Nevertheless, in act, there is an interplay between the three parts of the arm—no one part is entirely severed from the others.

Now the purpose of vibrato is to intensify feeling, and thus it must correspond and be used in accordance with the other aspects of feeling, i.e. phrasing and stress on individual notes and key points in groups of notes. Arbitrary use of vibrato is like a jagged edge in a pencil drawing where the arm has been accidentally jerked; truly used it is like the controlled brush of the Chinese landscape painter who uses a thicker line to accentuate a significant part of his subject. Vibrato is the violinist's strongest single weapon in affecting the feelings.

This can be seen in caricature if, in the following example from the slow movement of the Mozart G major Concerto, we virtually omit vibrato from the first five notes, picking out the emotional

stress only on the quaver E. A thousand similar instances could be quoted showing how vibrato contributes to shape in music.

We can readily see the importance of this privilege if we reverse the situation and play the E without vibrato whilst exaggerating it on the previous four notes. The result is an obvious mockery of

music. And there is another important point: the intensity of the vibrato on the E only has real effect if it starts at the very beginning of the note. Such an immediate tremor has the same quality as a catch in the breath and the beat of the heart from a feeling of awe, wonder or suspense. It can be represented diagrammatically as above. It is one of the greatest weaknesses of vibrato that it is rarely made to

 start at the first impact of the note, and thus much potential intensity is lost. Later in the same movement, interest is again held by immediate vibrato at the places marked by crosses. And even in notes of shorter duration, as in the opening of the D major Concerto, intensity of tone is lost unless vibrato starts at the moment of impact.

It is obviously as important, then, to study the relationship of vibrato to phrasing as it is to study it from the point of view of correct mechanics. Both work together to one end. So often, lack of musical understanding or bad mechanics causes the vibrato to swell out as a note progresses, just as the bow lacks an immediate bite and weighs heavily at its mid-point. A teacher should set out to show the great power a sensitive use of vibrato has over the feelings, and to dispel all idea that its lack can be compensated by force from the right arm. If vibrato were to be regarded as one third of the whole act of playing, players might be encouraged to regard it with respect from the first crucial moments the fingers touch the fingerboard.

19

PORTAMENTO AND FEELING

OF ALL the resources open to the violinist by which he may express emotion, portamento, moving gradually into a note from above or from below, is the most difficult to discuss in words. Feeling is typified by movement; without movement we are in the realm of the accurate and the predictable, which, as we know, is death to art. This is why we have spoken of variability in vibrato, movement in the body, movement in the flux of the breath, movement towards the head of a phrase, and why we are speaking now of movement in the approach to or away from a single note.

Yet in a way it is the most obvious way for a human being to express feeling. The concerted sound of the football crowd is nothing but the rise and fall of feeling—from it we can tell the history of the game. And the innumerable possible inflections of the simple words 'Oh no' tell us of the feelings those words may express. A poet reciting his verse, uncommitted to exact notation, has, in this sense, the fullest power in the field of sound; and after him the singer, because though committed to notation, he is expressing feeling through words and naturally approaches his song as though he were speaking it. From the singer downwards is a whole range of instruments, all capable in varying degrees of a natural capacity for moving gradually from one note to another, and according as that potential diminishes, losing the power of feeling to some extent. Thus there are certain instruments such as the oboe, the trumpet and the pianoforte, devoid of the deepest levels of feeling. Their quality is more associated with the head (oboe) or the passions (the trumpet), though we do not thereby discount feeling in them—the pianoforte, though essentially a percussive instrument, has a wide range of sensibilities. But it is the bowed strings that come nearest to the human voice. They have a continuous flow of sound, they can make vibrato and they are capable of the gradual approach to a note we call portamento. Unlike the voice, without specific emotion suggested by words, the string player is more concerned with an intuitive grasp of the music itself. Abstracted from words or any indicated emotional colouring, music may be less definable, but it is still essentially expressed feeling, and portamento is a powerful factor in that feeling, as we may see in any folk music of the world.

Portamento is not new in music, of course. It was one of the 'vanities' that crept into Gregorian chant, and in the middle of the seventeenth century in France, the fluid movements of the voice, (ornaments called *agrements*) bore the name 'port de voix', literally carrying of the voice; they were, according to a writer of the time 'befitted to move the soul powerfully'. In England such decorations were called *graces,* and were mainly slides and oscillations of pitch around one note. But the gradual emancipation of the violin from the voice led to the development of its own technique; and in any event the historical movement was away from the grace and fluency of the embellishment to a purity of classical line and form. So that by the time of Bach, ornaments could be represented as clearly articulated notes. There was none of the earlier florid sliding, and feeling became subdued within a firmer framework. In the slow movement of the Bach Double Concerto, for example, there is no trace of such ornaments. But there is no more intense feeling in the whole of music than in that particular movement, and we cannot suppose that it would have been played at the time with clinical accuracy; feeling must have been expressed by the player through an inner fluidity, vibrato and certainly the natural 'inaccuracies' involved through the shift from finger to finger. In the following passage:

such shifting at the right places allows a sensitivity that could never be achieved by the hand staying in one position: And in this passage, a sense of yearning comes of the delicate move into the quaver

B at the place indicated. But such places as this in one page of music are few, and the degree of movement so slight as to discountenance the use of the term 'portamento' at all.

The later classical framework, it would suggest, has no need for any such nuances: few ornaments are written and to all intents and purposes we have clear articulated notes. But the basic rise and fall inherent can never be lost in music. It falls and it rises in

hope and despair. In the Beethoven Romance in F precise articulation of each note would be death on a stringed instrument; perhaps what happens defies definition, but at the indicated places that precision gives way and life is injected. In the first small portamento the fourth finger slides, giving a clean articulation on the low F. In the second there is an example of the unique gift of the stringed instrument in being able to approach the new note from the note below the shift, giving a cleanly articulated C quaver.

Later, as the gates of romanticism began to open, the desire to transcend literalness increased, and with it, naturally, the need to express emotion through portamento. Though this is still not written as an instruction in the music, the Brahms Sonatas are clearly full of places where, with notes played mechanically, hitting each accurately on the head, the feeling and spirit of the

music is dead. In the places indicated in the examples (Brahms' Sonata in D minor), a considerable increase is needed in the amount of portamento used compared to the Beethoven example—it now becomes an integral part of the whole effect of

movement, vibrato and phrasing, all of which aim at affecting the heart. We are, relatively speaking, playing from the heart.

In all our examples, however, the concern is to keep feeling alive, and our judgment can only be regulated by what is known as 'good taste'. How much do we allow in Bach, how much in Beethoven, and what limit to put on Brahms? It seems strange that our success in this field can be put at the door of 'good taste'. Good taste is a point of restraint, a reverence for the right thing and a call upon the refined understanding of the player. And in music a solecism is more easily committed through portamento than through any other one thing—it can turn feeling into vulgar sentiment in a moment. Moreover, what is 'good taste' fluctuates from generation to generation and from period to period, and a musician is inevitably coloured by the spirit of his time, however it may be judged in retrospect.

Despite this, without portamento or a like movement of the

fingers so sensitive as to be undefinable, violin tone is lifeless. It may be the last thing we can teach, but it is also the first thing that was ever heard in nature's music, in the wind blowing through the branches and in man's struggle to express his feelings to his fellows.

20

WHAT IS AN INSTRUMENT?

THE ETYMOLOGY of the word 'instrument' (Latin, *instruere*, 'to build, construct; set in order, to teach') tells us that when we use an instrument we are in some ways concerned with creating order. Order is harmonious relationship of parts which gives rise to a sense of beauty, and it exists in the playing of music, in all crafts, and in sport. All these activities have three elements, the ordered shape of what is finally presented, the instrument that transmits this order, and the creative power at the source, that is the man himself. In a beautiful garden we have its order, the implements used, and the creative energy of the artist. In a sport like tennis we have the ordered behaviour of the ball, the racket, and the controlling force behind the racket; and in such a sport it is transparent that the correct behaviour of the ball is largely dependent on a perfectly fashioned racket.

But we have said that the activating force is always the man himself. On a higher level Man is also the tool of a superior Being—a tool being used in the perfecting of a cosmic plan. This is the drama of his life on earth. The vital forces he possesses are on loan, so to speak, so that he may use them to this end. In this sense Man is himself an *instrument*. Now if we look at that instrument we see that the physical body performs actions at the behest of invisible forces within him, and, as we saw in an earlier chapter, these forces are the ideas, the feelings and the willed intentions or energy. But they are, we also said, imperfect—each man uses his resources in an imperfect manner. Thus, since the musical instrument he plays is merely an extension of himself as a big instrument, it is inevitable that the small one he uses will carry all the imperfections of the bigger one, that it will be a direct reflection, on all levels, of what he as a person is.

The correspondence between the two instruments goes further. On the deepest level sound is the universal geometriser. All things vibrate at a given frequency, and sound, used consciously, can penetrate back through to the deepest levels and stimulate every part of man's being. The power of music is enormous, as we may see in the phenomenon of the glass shattered by a sympathetic frequency and in the Eastern mantra. (This subject has been discussed fully in the author's book *The Hidden Face of Music*.) In fact, men are essentially musicians moving to a knowledge of this power through sound manipulation, a process that can only come about through man's mastery over himself. It is not surprising, therefore, that the whole process is expressed in the human form of the violin, and in the anthropomorphic names of its parts. Not only do we find the 'bell', 'back', 'ribs', 'waist', 'neck', but the sound-post in French is called *l'âme* 'the soul', and in German *Stimme*, 'the voice'.

Because man is moving towards his own self-perfection, and because his instrument reflects him totally, it is not surprising that truly perfect and finished performances, despite the thousands of trained musicians in the world, are so rare. Is it not logical that if the small instrument needs to be made perfectly by a master-craftsman, and then needs to be perfectly tuned, the player himself, the bigger instrument, must also be perfect? Players reveal themselves through their instruments. Excesses in one area and weaknesses in another show themselves willy-nilly; and no two players are alike in the permutation of their qualities. To be involved in playing a stringed instrument is truly a privilege, for every step taken is a step towards mastery of self. And the raw material is unchanging—clarity of head, sensitivity of feeling, and immediacy of will—all working towards a potential harmony expressing itself through the physical body. These are the four necessary elements which when co-ordinated make either the small or big instrument powerful through wholeness.

Is it any wonder, then, that the violin, after a continual unconscious shaping towards embodiment in human form, ended also with four strings. Four, symbolically, is order through stability, seen in the physical world as North, East, South, West, or in the four elements, fire, air, water, earth. Is there any wonder too, that we find the string quartet so completely satisfying, for three seems to lack body, and five is one too many for clarity. Man, as we have seen, is basically *four* parts, not three, for in the end, nothing is possible without the physical world, without the physical body. We can see this too in the most basic of rhythms, our common time, four beats in a bar, because this is the relationship of our breathing and our heart-beat: there are 18 breaths per minute to 72 heart-beats per minute—a ratio of one to four.

Everywhere there is a conscious and an unconscious striving for perfection. The very form of the violin reached its term of perfection in its capacity to express technical clarity, feeling, and sheer power. A violinist seeks the finest instrument because he wants his instrument to respond in all three ways. The listener seeks a performance of the greatest beauty, and this, as we have said, means a harmonious relationship of these three parts. If the truth of this is seen by a student, he may have a new relationship with his instrument. But if he stops half way, and on leaving college gives up the quest, playing arbitrarily at the point he has reached, he has in a sense decided to die. To live, he must go on distilling perfection from his effort, using his instrument as a mirror of himself.

Now the same important concept of *work*—the shaping into order—is found not only in the word 'instrument' but also in two other words central to music. Both these words imply work: they are *organ* and *opera*. (Organ is from the Latin *organum* from the

Greek *organon*, 'instrument, tool', which is related to *ergon*, 'work'; and opera is from the Latin *opera*, neuter plural of *opus*, from the Sanskrit *apas*, 'work, religious act'.) Organum, historically, is the first step away from the hitherto unbroken tradition of monody towards the complexities of a harmonic structure and order. The organ, named after it, with all its keys embracing that system at the disposal of the musician, and finally all the stops embracing all possibilities of sound difference, became one great instrument of worship—work to the glory of God. And opera denoted in the past man's inner psychological work to find harmony within himself: this is apparent in the stories of operas, which were all originally based on myths to do with conflicts within his soul.

But there is a strange twist in this idea of work in the words 'instrument', 'organ', and 'opera'. The work on the stage became a *play*—a *player* presents the stories. And the musician who worships through his music at the organ becomes the *player* of that organ; in fact any instrument is *played*, as opposed to worked. What is the meaning, then, behind this play on words? Surely it lies in the fact that a man's life, in so far as it is tragic, is 'the play of the Gods'. but that through his work upon himself he can rediscover a sense of play within himself which resolves this apparent contradiction. The *work* necessary is the one of inner construction, the harmonising of parts. When a musical instrument is controlled, and order has been established, then it can be *played* in a true sense of the word—effort disappears and spontaneity appears. So when a student picks up his instrument to work, let him remember the overruling idea—that play is the reward and end of work.

CODA: IN DEFENCE OF SIMPLICITY

WHEN WE SEE with the eyes of a child, we do so immediately and without judgment. A man is a man, a tree is a tree. We actually feel something real about the thing we see, some fundamental quality in the man or in the tree. Then our leaders teach us to judge the man on a variety of moral issues, and our science books tell us the measurable facts about the tree. Each additional fact and judgment is a moving away from fundamental truth towards error, and error (Latin, *errare*,) simply means to wander or stray.

Any kind of activity is like this. There are so many personal judgments about a given thing—'personal' indicates the need to be different in the sense of an egotistic identity—that original simple truths are lost. In the field of science, for instance, personal theories held tenaciously for a time have countermanded each other in quick succession. Truth here is for ever changing. Science has seen a movement away from the intuitively experienced knowledge of the ancient civilisations to a science of a different ilk, rooted in empiricism and senses and personal competitiveness. By the same token, a man scarcely ever retains the enthusiasm for life he had as a child. Once he begins to measure life in terms of what is advantageous to him and starts to assimilate complex data about it, his eye of wonder becomes blurred by non-seeing.

We can see this error vividly in the image of the plain piece of paper which has been screwed up, because the *plex* part of the word *complex* means 'folds' (Latin, *plicare*, 'fold, wind together', from which also the word 'complicate'). What we are really seeing in the image of the ball of paper is something which has been made complex by being folded, so as to almost lose its original identity. And the more folds there are the less it will resemble that identity. But it is the same paper: in unfolding it we are simply unfolding the complexity to return to its simplicity.

The same principle applies to learning how to play an instrument. There are many personal judgments, many 'isms', and much apparent increasing complexity through greater and greater technical feats. But those feats are dependent upon the correct working of the basic simple truths. They are few, and they are ruthlessly effective; but the return is like going back through a labyrinth, the labyrinth of error and arbitrariness, and the return journey is not so easy as the outward one: it is easy to screw the paper up but not so easy to eradicate the folds.

So that when the term *simplicity* is used, what is implied is a possible recovery of simple truths. Thus, our aim is not to acquire information but to re-educate—that is, to draw out these basic buried truths. Most students have to make this return at some point in their training if they are to become efficient players. And this does not apply solely to those who are aiming to make music their profession: it applies to any level of making music. The simple basic truths are the ground of professional technique and amateur pleasure.

Now when the basic truths have been established we find the whole operation of playing becomes more simple. It feels more simple, it comes more easily to us. It is more like the play of the child, bouncing along without restraint. We do not *work* music. Music is *played*; and there is a strong affinity between simplicity and playfulness. But fear, inertias of the body and arbitrary technique all stand in the way and produce difficulty.

How, it may be asked, is it possible to be certain what are these simple truths that, we claim, are able to cut through the legacy of error? Ultimately, of course, each man has only his own decision, his own power of discrimination. Nevertheless, in this book and the earlier one, there has been a serious attempt to take science and psychology back to bare essentials, to unfold the folded paper and to make playing as simple as the revealed paper. We have studied the question of balance, and economy of control in the body and right hand; we have seen how all aspects of technique depend upon such economy; we have seen how gripping and forcing kill control, and we have advocated an opposite concept of 'let it happen'; we have studied the relationship of the two sides of the body, especially in terms of the tension embodied in the tautened bow and the tautened strings; we have studied the different function of the parts of the arm and the close relationship between music and breathing. If these concepts alone were to be the foundation of a new approach, most errors would begin to unfold naturally.

It may be asked 'What is the use of such ideas in teaching a child when they are obviously beyond his understanding?' The answer is of course that a child need not be burdened by ideas: he can be approached at his own level of understanding, the one of pure physical movement. To this he can respond because his body, as soon as it moves, urges to play; and this means that any aspect of technique can be turned into a game, whether it be the relationship of right and left, balance through movement, or the correspondence of gesture to the music. Such demands upon the body present great problems to the adult but are perfectly natural to the child. Intellectual explanations are necessary later when a player needs to be satisfied on that level, when he needs to see the logic of what he does. Such initial play, the development of the sense of play as opposed to struggle during the first few years, encourages and establishes the first great truth about playing—that technique has been perfected only when all sense of effort has been transcended and it has become child's play.

The danger facing a child is that he is pushed to 'get on' and is given far too many notes to learn before the simple truths have been allowed to take root. Thus, malfunctioning of the body and end-gaining causes arbitrariness and takes him gradually further and further into habitual error. Nothing in the world is difficult.

Men make difficulty. Difficulty arises through complexity; that is, the constant folding in the wrong direction. Once a man starts to reverse the process and to be a specialist in *undoing* error, he can become simple again. A violinist can then play with the spirit of the child, and will begin to realise how simple it all might have been from the beginning.

INDEX

Atlas bone, 21, 22
Attention, 96, 99

Balance, 17, 18, 20–2
Baroque period, and the bow, 60, 61
Body, its inertia, 19–21; its wisdom, 19; participation in playing, 17, 18, 20–2, 76–80; man's need of, 120
Bow, and the upper arm, 24–30; little finger on, 36–40; spontaneous bounce, 38, 39, 44–58; true control of, 36–42, 45–8; and right arm, 28, 41, 42; sense of resistance with string, 31, 32, 42, 58; differences in old and present-day bow, 59–61; co-ordination with left-hand, 70–3; conservation of, 74; and violin as in dance, 78, 79; and breathing, 104–6; bow-hair, 33–5
Bow-hair, importance of angle of, 33–5
Breathing, a universal activity, 100; element of doubt in playing, 101, 102; inner-breaths, 103–6: its dual function, 107; art and breath, 108

Child, play of, 122; method of work, 124

Civilisation, its effect upon sense of rhythm, 98
Control, of bow, true and false, 36, 42, 44; in left hand, 68
Co-ordination, of left and right, 70, 71
Crossing strings, danger in, 34

Dance, its use to the player, 78
Dynamics, and the spontaneous bounce of the bow, 50

Elbow, in plane of arm, 28
Eyes, danger of fixing, 86–7

Fingers, flexible hold on bow, 37, 38; control on bow, 46–8; of left hand, 42; and guide notes, 63; 'walking' the fingers, 64; thumb of left hand, 66–8
Feeling, 15, 16; in vibrato, 110–11; and portamento, 114, 115
Four-fold man, 120

Gesture, in playing, 76–83

Heel, difficulty of control at, 36–9

Imagination, its relation to technique, 88–94
Instrument, defined, 118; man as an instrument, 118–21

Knees, in balance, 21
Knuckles, of left hand, 42, 64

Left hand, its function, 28; co-ordination with bow, 70, 71, 74, 75
Left side, 28; its abuse and true use, 41, 42; symbolically, 70; its function in action, 80
Legato, problem of, 38, 39
Let, principle of, 19, 20
Little finger, and bow control, 36–40

Movement, gift of man, 17; in feet, 79
Music stands, danger of, 85, 86

Plane of arm, 33
Play, sense of play in the bow, 50, 51; its relationship to work, 121; its relationship to simplicity, 123, 124
Portamento, defined, 113; historically, 114; examples, 115–16
Posture, general, 20–3; and music stands, 85
Power, true source of in arm, 30, 31

Resistance, a sense of between bow and string, 31, 32, 42, 58
Rhythm, definition of, 96; the art of, 97, 98; effect of civilisation upon, 98
Right arm, 28; its abuse and true use, 41, 42; symbolically, 70; its function in action, 80

Shoulder, need for freedom in, 26–8
Simplicity, of child's vision, 122; need to recover, 123
Singer, related to the violinist, 30–2, 92
Sound, power of, 119
Speed, and spontaneous bouncing of bow, 50
Spontaneous bounce, 38, 39, 44–53; and baroque bow, 60, 61
Staccato, key to all staccato, 44, 45

Technique, and imagination, 88–91
Tension, correct and incorrect, 96, 97; and rhythm, 99
Thought, 15, 16, 28
Thumb, of right hand, 38; of left hand, 66–8
Three-fold, nature of man, 15, 24; in a player, 30, 31, 119, 120; in vibrato, 110; in artistic activity, 118
Thrown-staccato, 45, 46

Upper arm, use and abuse of, 24–31

Vibrato, different types of, 109; correct action; use in phrasing, 111, 112

Weight, in right arm, 42
Will, 16, 24, 28, 41
Work, as making order, 121; in relation to play, 121
Wrist, and angle of bow, 33–5; in holding instrument, 66–8